WHAT IS PROCESS THEOLOGY?

What Is
Process Theology?

by

Robert B. Mellert

PAULIST PRESS
New York / Paramus / Toronto

Library of Congress
Catalog Card Number: 74-28933

ISBN: 0-8091-1867-X

Published by Paulist Press
Editorial Office: 1865 Broadway, N.Y., N.Y. 10023
Business Office: 400 Sette Drive, Paramus, N.J. 07652

Printed and bound in the
United States of America

CONTENTS

PREFACE

During the 1960's a remarkable revival of the thought of the contemporary American process philosopher, Alfred North Whitehead, took place in the studies and dens of graduate students in philosophy. It was remarkable because, although he died in 1947, Whitehead was only a few cards in the library catalogue until, during the past decade and continuing into the present, literally shelves of books have been written explaining his thought, interpreting it, and applying it to a variety of areas.

One of the most fruitful applications of Whiteheadian thought has been in the area of theology. In fact, the study of "process theology" in departments of religion and theology has perhaps equaled, if not exceeded, the study of process thought in departments of philosophy where it all started. This, despite the fact that Whitehead was no theologian, and indeed, after a short period of curiosity, he sold all his theology books and never returned to the subject.

Today every respectable graduate school of theology has its process theologian, or at least someone able to teach the subject adequately. And consequently, more and more people engaged in religious education— religion teachers, seminarians, catechetics coordinators, clergy, and interested laymen—have heard about process theology and perhaps have seen references to it. But a comfortable familiarity with what it is all about has, for most of them, been an elusive goal.

This little book is written as a reply to my many friends who have asked me, in the midst of conversations going in various directions, "What is process theology?" I have never really known how to respond to that question briefly and politely. Surely there is no way to reply adequately, short of three credit hours or a select bibliography. Now, at least, I can tell them where they might get started.

It is my hope that this volume will help to "bridge the gap" between the professional philosophers and theologians and the many other persons who are looking for a basic familiarity with process theology but who do not have the time to struggle with the complexities of the process system as a whole. There is, I feel, a great need for such a volume. Once process philosophers and theologians have mastered the jargon and technical intricacies of Whitehead's thought, they generally prefer to share the intellectual excitement of their work with each other, rather than to attempt repeated explanations for the benefit of the uninitiated. Thus, journal articles abound since the early 1960's, but only fleeting references are found in the more widely circulated religious magazines. Hopefully, the 1970's will see a better dissemination of this mode of thought to a broader range of interested persons.

There are already indications that this is beginning to take place. Graduate students have received their degrees in Whiteheadian studies and are now teaching undergraduates. Institutes have been conducted to acquaint clergy and laity. And recently two volumes of collected writings have appeared in paperback: *Process Philosophy and Christian Thought*, edited by Delwin Brown, Ralph James and Gene Reeves,[1] and *Process*

Theology, edited by my friend and former teacher, Ewert Cousins.[2]

My own work here will attempt to simplify as best I can the foundations of process philosophy and to suggest ways in which I find it helpful for explaining Christian thought. My own orientation in Christianity has been in the Roman Catholic tradition, and this may in part determine the topics I choose and the ways in which I treat them. However, this should not dissuade readers of other Christian traditions because the differences are, for the most part, negligible for the beginner in process theology.

A greater danger lies in over-simplification and distortion, and I am very much aware that in "watering down" Whitehead for the popular palate, I may in fact destroy the real flavor of his philosophy. This would be a grave disservice both to Whitehead and to my own conviction that process thought has a very important contribution to make to our age of critical religious rethinking and reconstruction.

Nevertheless, process philosophers and theologians must not be allowed to talk only to each other. Others, too, must be initiated, and they must begin with simpler things. If this book, as a simple thing, spurs someone on toward the greater things, or if it simply convinces someone that there might be greater things than he had previously conceived of in his theology, then I shall have achieved the goal I have set for myself and my efforts will be adequately rewarded.

Finally, I wish to express my gratitude to the numerous persons who have helped me and encouraged me in this work. I wish to mention especially the University of Dayton's Summer Research Institute, which provided me with a grant to begin this project; Rev.

Matthew Kohmescher, S.M., my department chairman; and two personal friends, Sister Carol Gaeke, O.P., and Ellen Simonetti, who graciously read the manuscript and suggested many improvements.

I

WHY SOMETHING NEW?

The term "process philosophy" has taken on a special meaning in the past two decades of American thought. Although many philosophers in history have written from a process perspective, the term today is reserved for a particular school of thought centered around the works of Alfred North Whitehead, whose philosophical writings spanned the two decades of the 1920's and 1930's and the two countries of England and the United States. From its inception, but especially in the past fifteen years, Whitehead's process philosophy has been attracting students and scholars at numerous universities to study and elaborate upon his basic insights. Recently a special institute and a professional journal have been established to aid the growth of Whiteheadian studies in this country and abroad.

What are the origins of Whitehead's thought, and why is he attracting so much attention today? What is his value for theology in this age of radical thinking? Is Whitehead just one more passing fad, or does his philosophy provide a solid, durable basis for understanding and interpreting the Christian faith?

The roots of process thought, like most of Western philosophy, can be traced back to the Greeks. The most ancient of the specifically "process" thinkers is probably Heraclitus. Unfortunately, the ideas of Heraclitus and his contemporary Parmenides are available to us only in a few fragments, and these provide merely a hint of their thought. We are told that Heraclitus once observed that one could never step into the same river twice (because by the time one steps into it the second time the water has already moved downstream), and that the basis of reality was change and flux. This idea was in sharp contrast with Parmenides, who suggested in his poem about nature that "being" was prior to "becoming," and that underlying every change was some more fundamental reality that endured. By a fateful choice of history, Parmenides became the father of metaphysics and the basis for later Greek philosophy, while Heraclitus was largely ignored. As a result, the thrust of Greek thought, and most of Western thought thereafter, was derived from the static concepts of "being," "substance," and "essence," rather than the more dynamic concepts of "becoming," "process," and "evolution."

Whitehead likewise acknowledged his indebtedness to the Greeks, especially to Plato. Indeed he once remarked that all of Western philosophy is a series of footnotes to Plato. Although Plato is not a process philosopher, his thought can be reconciled with a process perspective. This is exactly what Whitehead did. *How* he reconciled them is not as important to us here as the knowledge that contemporary process thought, following Whitehead, is both processive in character and Platonic in spirit. When we discuss some of the basic concepts of Whiteheadian philosophy in the next chapter, the implications of these facts will become more clear.

Whitehead's increasing importance today in America can be attributed to the fact that his philosophy arises out of the Hellenic tradition and emerges in an age of rapid change. Because he is thoroughly a part of our Western tradition, his insights are not alien to our cultural presuppositions. For all the difficulty of understanding his thought, he can be more readily grasped and appreciated by Western man than can, for example, Oriental thought, because Whitehead's thought is built upon what is already familiar to us in our own Western culture and tradition.

But today there is developing a certain discontent with our culture and its tradition, and a certain suspicion regarding its capacity for radical change. There is the feeling that our institutions, both civil and ecclesiastical, and even the thinking that inspired them, are inadequate and insufficient to meet the future. Doubts of this kind are fundamentally philosophical doubts about the ability of our philosophies to deal with change as a fundamental category of reality. Our philosophical heritage is being questioned in the light of a rapidly changing culture.

One of the reasons for this radical questioning is that the very way in which we perceive reality has been changing. Until very recent times we were quite content and intellectually satisfied with the way Parmenides viewed the universe. There was an underlying stability to our institutions, our culture, and our lives. But in recent years we are being confronted more forcefully with the fact of change, and with the fact that the rate of change is itself increasing.

All of this rapid changing has created for us a new perception of reality. No longer is reality fundamentally stable, with change being merely an accidental alteration of its makeup. Today reality itself is experienced as being in constant flux, so that the basic category of reality is process, not stability. In a more sophisticated way we have returned to the insight of Heraclitus: we cannot step into the same river twice because our world is not the same world twice. Reality is a process.

There is also another way in which our perception of reality has been changing. Because of new means of communication and rapid methods of transportation the world seems much smaller to us now than it did just a couple of generations ago. Today, a political event in the Middle East has instant repercussions on the stock market in New York, thus changing the financial plans of people around the world. Our astronauts, relying on the precision technology of a team of scientists, can travel to the moon and back in half the time it took our grandparents to cross the Atlantic to settle in this country, and the event is seen live on television sets around the world. We experience more than ever before the interrelatedness of the people and things in our universe and the interdependence of reality as a whole.

We experience this relational character of reality also in our heightened sensitivity to the natural environment and to the historical context out of which things emerge. Knowing whether a child comes from the suburbs or the ghetto, from a loving family or a broken home, gives us certain insights into his conduct and suggests certain methods of helping him mature. Or, to use a different example, we learn to understand and interpret certain events in history or expressions in literature according to the context in which they arose. To know something requires knowledge of its environment and context, because nothing exists in isolation. Every bit of reality is essentially related to the totality of reality in its own unique way, and it depends upon the rest of reality for its origin, meaning and value.

Whitehead was very conscious of this interrelatedness of reality, and it is an essential part of his philosophical theory. In fact, he chose to call his philosophy the "philosophy of organism" because he based it upon a theory of the real relatedness of things. That is why his thinking tends toward integrating and synthesizing, rather than individualizing and classifying. Reality is first of all a complex unity, or organism, and each element in that unity is itself an organismic unity. One of his purposes for doing philosophy is to suggest how they all interrelate. The concept of organism provides the model for understanding this relatedness and integration of all reality.

Because Whitehead is a part of Western tradition and takes it into account in the development of his own thought, and because he gives us a philosophical system that is essentially processive in character and relational in structure, his philosophy of process and organism seems more relevant to contemporary needs than any of the "substance philosophies" that are more common in this tradition. This is the basic advantage of Whitehead. Whereas most of Western thought is formulated in static, individuating and non-temporal concepts, Whitehead adds the temporal and integrative dimensions that make his system dynamic, holistic and four-dimensional. This is the reason why he finds it necessary to invent a new vocabulary to explain his philosophical concepts. The next chapter will be devoted to defining and explaining some of the most significant Whiteheadian terms.

The reasons that make Whiteheadian thought important for philosophy also make it relevant for theology. No institutions are more tied to their respective traditions than religious institutions, and nowhere has the accelerating rate of change been more upsetting and misunderstood than in the Christian churches of the last two decades. This has been particularly true in the Catholic Church, which has guarded its individuality more tenaciously than its Protestant brethren, and which is still in the throes of the radical (and reactionary) renovation that Vatican Council II was supposed to have resolved.

There is in many Christian, and especially Catholic circles today a tendency to blame theology for the confusion and to demand a simple, unquestioning act of faith. According to such thinking, any attempt to formulate a theological perspective according to Whiteheadian—or any—thought is to continue the confusion and frustrate the return to a peaceful Christian orthodoxy. But an appeal to faith is not a solution to intellectual problems, and an appeal to orthodoxy is simply an appeal to the *expression* of faith of the Christians of another era who formulated that orthodoxy. Faith is not a substitute for thought, and orthodoxy is not a substitute for either. Rather, faith is the immediate occasion for challenging and developing thought so that it can better integrate itself with reality as a whole. This is precisely the function of theology. According to the old Latin expression, theology is *fides quaerens intellectum* (faith seeking understanding). Although this expression goes back to the early traditions of Christian theology, it is still applicable today. Faith does seek understanding; it does not replace understanding. And the understanding it seeks must be discovered in conjunction with the most enlightened perception of reality available to it in a particular historical epoch.

Whitehead is becoming important for Christian theology because he provides us with such an enlightened perception of reality. He sees reality in a way that makes sense to our contemporary mind. Those who, like Whitehead, see reality in terms of process and organism, and who likewise believe in a special revelation that comes to man in the Christian tradition, will seek to integrate what they believe with what they see. This is precisely what Augustine did with the philosophy of Plato and what Thomas Aquinas did with the philosophy of Aristotle. Each sought to integrate his Christian faith with the best available understanding of reality as a whole. This is the fundamental task of theology. It is the immediate task of any believer who thinks about what he believes, and who lives on the basis of his beliefs.

To suggest that we ought to return to the "original faith" and ignore theology is to reject any attempt to think about our faith in our contemporary context or to integrate what we believe with how we live in our contemporary world. To suggest that we ought to return to "orthodoxy" is to suggest that we can best express our faith today by disregarding the development of human philosophy subsequent to the original, or "orthodox" expression of that faith. Such suggestions are blind to the processive and contextual character of reality as a whole, where faith must ultimately find its meaning.

What process theologians are attempting to do is essentially the same as what Augustine and Thomas did: to express their Christian faith in the conceptual language of a philosophy that makes sense to their age. But can process theologians actually write a theology in the sense that Augustine and Thomas did? That is, can they truly integrate their philosophy with the beliefs of the Christian community and provide those beliefs with a credible foundation in reason?

To answer such questions, we must do some reflection on what we expect of a theology. First, it must be based upon a conviction that a particular person, event or tradition has a special revelatory significance for man. For Christian theology, that event is the person of Jesus and the tradition that has developed in his Spirit. Second, it must seek to understand that conviction in a coherent, consistent and relevant way. Here the Christian is free to choose whatever philosophical perspective can best integrate his faith with his view of reality as a whole. The perspective that he chooses will determine the way in which he expresses his faith. That is, his choice about a philosophy will determine the shape of his theology. Consequently, there can be many theologies endeavoring to explain the one faith. Unity in faith comes from a common belief in the revelatory significance of Jesus; plurality in theology comes from differing views regarding the nature of reality into which that faith must be integrated.

Process theology is a theology that uses processive and organismic models to explain the faith of Christians in the person of Jesus and the events and traditions that he has inspired. It is still theology in the traditional sense of "faith seeking understanding." But it is different from traditional theology in that it uses the process philosophy of Alfred North Whitehead (instead of Plato or Aristotle) to express and integrate that belief into our contemporary perception of reality —a perception which is increasingly sensitive to integration and change as the fundamental reality.

It is indeed a difficult task to "switch gears" from a theology based on static, spatial models alone, such as the *essence* of God, the *natures* of Christ, and the *substance* of bread and wine, to a theology that is concerned with spatio-temporal models, such as *change* in God, Christ *becoming* divine, and the on-going *process* of revelation. It is also difficult to change from an analytic approach, where one is constantly distinguishing among essentially different kinds of reality and the individual "beings" in each level of reality, to a more synthetic approach, where everything, including God, is ultimately explainable with one set of categories and is integrated with the reality of the whole. And yet, such concepts are not so strange to one who believes that God is alive and that religion ought to integrate and influence the dynamics of human living. Both Scripture and tradition contain much data to support the use of process models in the development of a Christian theology. Whether such a theology will ultimately find more acceptance among scholars and believers than the "substance theologies" of the past can only be tested by the passage of time.

II

SOME BASIC CONCEPTS

Alfred North Whitehead was a man of many interests and many talents. Born in England in 1861, he entered the intellectual life before the deluge of scientific knowledge and the age of specialization. As a result, he was able to pursue and develop an expertise in several fields in a way that is perhaps no longer possible for anyone today. His interests first took him into the realm of science, and he made important contributions in both physics and mathematics. Only later did he turn his attention to philosophy. Throughout his life he maintained a lively interest in the literary and the fine arts. In addition, he was always an avid student of history.

Such a broad range of interests gives Whiteheadian philosophy a rare richness. But this richness is the cause of difficulty for the reader of a narrower ken. To master Whitehead is a long, arduous task. Even a comfortable acquaintance can be difficult because of the new terminology that Whitehead formulates and the new meanings he sometimes gives to old terms. Without these precisions of vocabulary, however, his unique insights are in danger of being lost.[1]

Whitehead's basic insight is that reality is a series of interrelated becomings. How a thing *becomes* constitutes what a thing *is*. The process of becoming is more fundamental than the being that is achieved, and thus it is more important for philosophical study. It is perhaps interesting to note that the term "being" is actually a form of the verb, even though most philosophers use it as a substantive noun. To say that something is a "being" or has "being" is to attribute to it more than static reality. It is to infer a *continuous* existence in that reality through time. It is a being because it is be-ing. Because this temporal connotation has been lost in speaking philosophically about "beings," Whitehead prefers to speak philosophically about "becomings." In this way he wishes to emphasize the fundamental processive character of reality.

This insistence on the temporal dimension of reality requires that Whitehead formulate a vocabulary that can lure us out of our static representations of reality. If, for example, someone were asked to identify the smallest unit of reality, he would probably say "the tiniest bit of matter, an atom, or perhaps an electron." The problem with this answer is that we do not generally think of tiny bits of matter as *becomings*; we think of them as *beings*. Hence, to use bits of matter as the model for our philosophical understanding of the fundamental elements of reality is to freeze us into a static pattern of philosophical thought. Whitehead frees us from this kind of thinking by coining a new term: the fundamental elements of reality are *actual occasions* (which he sometimes calls *actual entities* or *occasions of experience*).

To enable us to understand what he means by this new term, Whitehead suggests a new model. Instead of bits of matter, we might better think of the basic units of reality as *moments of experience*. Moments of experience provide a more suitable model for understanding these fundamental elements of reality because they have a temporal thickness to them which bits of matter do not have. Thus, when we think of reality as consisting of moments of experience, we are conscious that reality is always becoming.

Another advantage of the "experience" model is that it demonstrates the essential interrelatedness of reality. A moment of experience cannot be thought of in isolation or as an independent entity. It is always an experience by someone of something, and it always requires antecedent experiences to give it meaning and relative importance. A moment of experience necessarily implies a reference to the world around it. Both process and interrelation are thus built into this model of reality, whereas they were only accidental to the old "bit of matter" model.

The concept of actual occasion is the central notion of Whiteheadian thought. Actual occasions, or "drops of experience," are the final real things of which the world is made, and there is no going behind them to find anything more real. All of reality, from God to the most trivial puff of existence, is explainable in terms of actual entities, and only in these terms. They are the only reasons for things. Outside of actual entities, there is nothing at all.

One clarification may be needed at this point. For Whitehead, experience need not be conscious experience. The latter belongs only to certain kinds of actual entities. Everything experiences: the balloon experiences relative air pressures; the rock experiences the earth upon which it rests. Experience is basic to all real things. It is the reason why reality is interrelated as well as processive in character.

The other fundamental type of entity in Whitehead's philosophy is called the *eternal object*. Eternal objects are pure possibilities. They are similar to Aristotle's universals or Plato's forms in that they are abstract. But they differ because they do have a real mode of existence in actual entities. They likewise have a reference to other eternal objects, because relatedness is a condition of organism even at the level of abstraction. Examples of eternal objects are colors, sounds, scents and geometric characters. They are required for nature but they do not emerge from it the way actual entities do. They appear and disappear in many different contexts, and yet whenever they appear they are always the same. However, they do not have an independent or ideal existence apart from the actualities in which they are manifested. They are merely possibilities available for actualization. Whitehead defines them as pure potentials for the specific determination of fact.

The way in which every actual occasion is the subject of experiences brings us to the third important concept, *prehension*. At first glance, this term may look like a misspelling of "apprehension." The similarity is not accidental. Both are derived from the Latin, meaning "to take." The word "apprehension" connotes a "taking hold of" something, understanding it, and finding its meaning. It is the action of a subject perceiving an object and evaluating its import for the future. However, before a subject can take hold of and understand an object in this sense, it must be related to that object. The fact of being related to something is more fundamental than a subjective perception of an object. Prehensions, says Whitehead, are the concrete facts of relatedness.

The fact of relatedness has a further implication

that is not contained in the word "apprehension," but which is essential to Whitehead's notion of "prehension." A child is related to his parents differently from the way in which his parents are related to him. Whereas parents are only externally influenced by their children, a child's very existence, his genetic inheritance, and parental influences during early childhood all help to determine how he is to mature and grow. He "takes" from his parents his very reality as an individual person. An emerging entity is similarly related to eternal objects and past actual entities in that these are the elements out of which the new entity is to become. Prehension, therefore, also indicates that the relatedness of these elements to the emerging actual entity is determinative because the relatedness constitutes the entire data available to that entity in its process of becoming. In the language of the Scholastic philosophers, a prehension would be roughly equivalent to a "real relation." That is, the relation of the things prehended to the subject prehending determines what that subject will become.

Another way of understanding "prehension" is in terms of "feeling." As an actual occasion or moment of experience emerges, it "feels" all the data available to it in its own universe. These are its prehensions. They can be of two kinds, physical or conceptual. Physical prehensions relate the emerging entity to the actual occasions of the immediate past that are within its scope and enable it to "feel" them. Conceptual prehensions are "feelings" of relevant eternal objects.

Every actual occasion prehends both physically and conceptually during the formation of its own unique synthesis. The more it prehends physically, the more it tends to repeat what it feels from the past; the more it prehends conceptually, the more novelty is introduced. It is important to emphasize again in this context that because a prehension is a determinative relationship, these "feelings" are not accidental additions or modifications of the actual entity (as "apprehension" would imply), but constitutive of it. An actual entity *is* what it *feels*.

Because an actual occasion is merely a drop of experience, we are generally conscious only of groups of actual occasions, or *nexūs* (plural of nexus). A nexus is a set of actual occasions experienced as related to each other. Sometimes it is called a society of occasions. The human body is a society of this type because the actual occasions of each part of the body are experienced as being spatially connected in the formation of a single body. An illustration of this kind of nexus might be a loosely crocheted garment, where the knots constitute the actual occasions and the connecting threads their relatedness. Man is, in addition, a serial nexus, i.e., a series of actual occasions, or a stream of personal experiences that can be traced through a definite period of history. A serial nexus might be described as a "motion picture" film, in which a rapid series of individual occasions of experience project movement.

The nexus is the way in which Whitehead explains the real connections of things in space and time. Moments of experience are intrinsically related to each other by prehensions to form nexūs. It is the real connections of things that we perceive, not the individual actual occasions. Our experience of reality is in terms of networks and patterns. Nothing is experienced alone. Each nexus is perceived in the context of a wider nexus, just as each element of a nexus emerges out of the environment of that nexus. Every part of reality is as we perceive it—a part of a larger whole.

These four terms—actual occasions, eternal objects, prehensions and nexūs—are the most important terms in the Whiteheadian vocabulary. We are now ready to explain how they fit together to form a philosophical perception of reality. The explanation will require the introduction of still more new terminology, but the new terms will be of lesser importance and will be more easily defined.

Each actual occasion emerges at a particular locus in time and space when that locus becomes the center of converging feelings, or prehensions. As it emerges it has its own particular *subjective aim*, which controls the becoming of that subject. This subjective aim is directed toward the particular satisfaction that the actual occasion seeks to achieve. An emerging occasion prehends its relevant data according to its subjective aim and gives it focus according to that satisfaction.

The key to how an actual occasion becomes lies in the interaction that takes place between the subject (actual occasion) prehending and the data (past occasions and/or eternal objects) being prehended. *How* this interaction takes place is determined by the *subjective form*, which is the particular mood or attitude by which the subject prehends a particular datum. There are many species of subjective forms. Examples are emotions, valuations, purposes, adversions, aversions and consciousness. While an actual occasion can have only one subjective aim, the subjective forms depend upon its prehensions. One occasion, therefore, can involve a number of subjective forms.

Every act of prehending has its subjective form, but not every prehension contributes its datum to the emerging occasion. This is the reason for distinguishing between positive and negative prehensions. A prehension whose datum is included as a constitutive aspect of the occasion is a positive prehension; one in which the datum is eliminated from feeling is called a negative prehension. This is why the new actual occasion is constituted by its prehensions of the past but it is not necessarily a mere repetition of the past. It can be constituted into a new and novel synthesis because it can prehend the elements of its past in different ways. In one sense, then, the past determines the present moment of experience, in that it is the only data available for the present; in another sense, the present moment of experience is free to determine how it is to become.

And yet, nothing of the past is ever really lost. Every actual occasion lives on, contributing its reality to the occasions that succeed it. This is the meaning of *objective immortality*. After the actual occasion achieves its subjective aim and reaches its own particular satisfaction, it perishes. That is, it can experience no longer. But it is not lost or annihilated, because it can still *be* experienced. It becomes an objective datum for future occasions to take account of, positively or negatively, in the continuance of process. As it is prehended, it is immortalized as a constitutive element of the nexūs of occasions that continue to "feel" its impact on history.

Because each actual occasion is its own unique synthesis of its past, each contributes its own actualization to the totality of reality. Each becomes part of the many, and adds itself to the complex environment that gives rise to a new occasion. The new occasion emerges by the unique way in which it objectifies, immortalizes and brings to a new unity the elements of its relevant past. When it achieves that satisfaction, it, too, perishes, clearing the way for the process to continue. In Whitehead's succinct phrase, "The many become one and are increased by one."[2]

This is what Whitehead means by *creativity*. It is the ultimate principle by which the multiplicity of relevant data become one actual occasion, illustrating the fact that it is the nature of things that the many enter into complex unity. The three ultimate notions, then, are creativity, many, and one.

The above description of the process by which an actual entity becomes explains both the processive character of reality and the essential integration of reality as a whole. It should be noted that at every level of Whiteheadian thought we are dealing with unities of pluralities in dynamic inter-relation. In the above analysis of actual occasions as moments of experience, we have been discussing reality at its smallest, or microscopic level. Even at this level the actual occasion, which is the smallest reality considered in process thought, is the unity of many prehensions. That is why actual occasions must themselves be understood as organisms.

On this point Whitehead's thought is essentially different from those philosophical traditions where the iscroscopic elements are bits of matter. The presupposition in the latter is that every unity can be further broken down into its components, which are also real. One finally arrives at an ultimate unit of reality—an electron, for example—which can then be described abstractly in terms of locus, function, quality and quantity, etc. For Whitehead, there are no such fundamental units of reality because reality is composed of moments of experience and not bits of matter. When a moment of experience is analyzed into its components, these components (prehensions) are not real apart from the moment of experience, or actual occasion itself, even though they contribute reality to that occasion. Actual occasions, which are the final real things of the universe, are thus unities, not units of reality. Hence, ultimate reality is organismic reality. It cannot be broken down for further analysis except by forsaking the realm of real things for the realm of abstraction.

By analogy, nexūs, or societies of actual occasions, are also organisms, because they are unities of more fundamental elements. Larger organisms are complex unities of smaller organisms. At the largest, or macroscopic level of reality the same pattern obtains. Reality as a whole is a complex unity of pluralities. Here, too, Whitehead's central notion is manifested. The many become one and are increased by one. Each group of smaller unities that occasions the emergence of a larger, more comprehensive unity adds to the total sum of organisms in reality and thus adds to reality itself. For this reason, the whole is greater than the sum of its parts because the whole is itself a new reality beyond the parts. Therefore, both in its processive character and in its relational structure, creativity is achieved when multiplicities give rise to new unities and are thereby increased by those unities.

This, in very brief outline, is the basic structure of Whitehead's thought. There are many other terms and concepts which have been purposely eliminated for the sake of simplicity. There are also many controversies regarding various aspects of the interpretation presented here, and these, too, have been set aside. Our main purpose has been merely to introduce the reader to

what is fundamental in process philosophy so that the
theological chapters which follow can be more fully and
positively prehended.

III

RELIGION

A few years ago, when a variety of liturgical changes were being introduced in their Church, many Roman Catholics suffered a severe crisis of faith. The Church as they knew it—with its Latin Mass and Benediction of the Blessed Sacrament—had changed beyond their recognition, and the readjustment to the "new Church"—with its guitar Masses and handshakes of peace—was very traumatic. There is something to be said for their appreciation of the old liturgy. It provided a sense of the mysterious and mystical that has been lost in the reforms. Hearing priests mumble a strange language and seeing the Eucharist in a gold casing surrounded by candles and flowers created an atmosphere that often generated profound religious feelings.

The new liturgy does not recapture that kind of experience, nor does it try. Sacraments are better instruments for evoking communitarian feelings than private feelings. Thus, the new liturgy attempts to create a new kind of religious experience, that of a community of Jesus' followers living and loving together in his name. The spirit of fellowship manifested at a liturgy which is prepared and executed with this purpose in mind becomes the sign of Christian charity and the motivating cause to carry it beyond the liturgical community to the world at large.

Both the mystical and the communitarian are authentic religious experiences and genuine forms of Christian prayer. The fact that today's liturgies emphasize the latter in no way minimizes the importance of the former. It merely indicates that the religious life of man requires more than simply participating at liturgies. The solitary figure bent in prayer in a quiet, darkened chapel, no less than the happy, youthful faces sharing a dialogue homily, inspires us to an appreciation of what the religious spirit in man is.

Numerous other kinds of experiences can also be appropriately called religious. These likewise emerge from time to time in private prayer and public worship. Theologians, psychologists and philosophers have all tried to catalogue these experiences. Examples include the experiences of transcendence, awe, insignificance, gratitude, acceptance by God, reverence, guilt, sense of obligation, and inner shame. Sometimes the experience is less obviously religious, such as that of wholeness, simplicity, and the unity of reality; of uniqueness, individuality, and power; of the fittingness and appropriateness of things; or of the moving together, transformation, and harmonization of particulars.[1] The number and kinds of religious experiences are almost infinite, probably because they are so unique and particular to those who have experienced them. Their degree of intensity likewise varies, from full-blown visions to fleeting moments of private recollection.

Whitehead's own appraisal is that religious experiences begin with personal occasions of solitude and extend to the universal. He writes that religion is what the individual does with his own solitariness.[2] This solitariness includes even the experience of feeling forsaken by God. From religion one learns to cope with himself and to take upon himself the burden of his own life. But this is only the negative side. The religious man also learns to appreciate reality and to be sensitive to it in a personal way. This is because religion deals with particular emotions and personalized purposes. There is a certain aesthetic character to its feeling for the world. Things have a certain value or worth beyond what they actually are, because they reveal mystery, beauty and meaning that can be understood in no other way. A man is thus taken beyond himself and provided with a way of prehending the universe.

What religion ultimately grasps, according to Whitehead, is this truth: "That the order of the world, the depth of reality of the world, the value of the world in its whole and in its parts; the beauty of the world, the zest of life, the peace of life, and the mastery of evil, are all bound together."[3] This occurs not accidently, but as a result of the creativity, the freedom, and the infinite possibilities that the universe manifests.

Because this statement of Whitehead is central to his idea of religion, and because some of the words carry a connotation peculiar to his thought, a few reflections may clarify his meaning. Order is not the same for Whitehead as it is for politicians. It is the refusal of the deadening influence of conformity and the tendency toward new forms and ordered novelty. Depth is the result of cumulative achievements of the world that make enrichment possible. Value, as particularized in every occasion of reality, reveals itself in continual interaction, promoting depth and destruction. Beauty is a central concept in Whiteheadian thought, because it defines "the one aim which by its very nature is self-justifying,"[4] and toward which the universe constantly strives. But the mere repetition of beauty can

become dull and uninteresting without adventure and
the zest of life urging it to new and exciting harmonies
and contrasts. Finally, peace is the "harmony of harmonies which calms destructive turbulence and com-
pletes civilization."[5] While not religious in themselves,
these insights into reality arise from the religious sensitivities of man and add an appreciation to the universe
that only religion can provide.

The basic religious insight, then, is that we can
know more than can be formulated in the abstract schema of science and philosophy.[6] This "extra knowledge"
comes from religion's intuition about the aims and purposes of things that are revealed in the wisdom of na-
-ture itself. It is not new factual data, but a new feeling,
or prehension of the old data. Thus, religion is always
saying more than science or philosophy about man and
his world, even though it is not privy to special information. Its "saying more" is not something that can be
proved or demonstrated; it can merely be pointed to,
felt, and appreciated. This is the sense in which one
might repeat with the Scholastic theologians that there
is a knowledge that comes from faith. It is a knowledge
that goes beyond the reasons of the mind to the sensitivities of the soul.

The desire of the religious man to preserve these
experiences has led to his repeated attempts to set down
his inspiration for the edification of others. This is the
origin of creeds and dogmas. They are testimony to
what religious experience can inspire in man's intuition,
and they reveal in retrospect the power and intensity of
religion in the history of man. The danger is that when
a man has no religious experiences of his own, he tends
to repeat those that have been handed down from
others in their creedal and dogmatic formulations. Reli-

gion that finds itself constantly relying upon these secondary sources has lost its original vitality and creativity. Dogmas that are merely repeated become rigid, abstract concepts that fail to inspire. They result in a narrowing of perspective and a sheltering of religion from its necessary commerce with the world, where new insights and inspirations are occasioned, and where new dogmas and creeds tentatively emerge.

Ideally, therefore, the solitariness that inspires religion in man extends beyond the individual to the universal. The values that are intuited in the formation of character in the private feelings of a man are not isolated from a more general picture of the world. Character requires that one's individuality merge with the universe. Ultimately, says Whitehead, "religion is world-loyalty."[7]

From what has been said above, it is readily apparent that the religious spirit is very important to Whitehead and to his way of thinking. Its importance is not in any unique claim to truth, but in its contributions to rationality as a whole. Its chief contribution is its familiarity with the particular, and in this way it is the essential complement to philosophy. Philosophy by itself is always speculative and general, and as such is always plagued with the suspicion of inapplicability. Religion frees philosophy from this suspicion because it is "the translation of general ideas into particular thoughts, particular emotions, and particular purposes."[8] At the same time, religion is itself always interested in the universal, because the generalities of philosophy give some coherence to the particularities of emotion and feeling that belong to the data of religion. There is, then, a mutual enrichment. Philosophy needs the data of religious experience in order to remain sensitive to the particu-

lar, and religion needs philosophy to modify it, ratio-
nalize it, and fit it into a wider context.

Science is the third corner of this triangle, and it,
too, helps to support rationality as a whole. Like religion, science also contributes something to philosophical speculation. Its contribution is data—not necessarily a different set of data from that available to religion,
but a different way of looking at that data. Science is
concerned with what is perceived, and how these perceived things can be integrated with rational thought in
a harmonious way. Religion is concerned with achieving some kind of harmony between rationality and the
sensitive reactions of the perceiver to what is perceived.
Religious considerations always deal with the particular
feelings that data evoke. When certain sciences, such as
psychology, study particular feelings, they do their work
in an objective fashion, i.e., with other people's emotions, not their own. How particular feelings transform
the experiencing subject, and how they ultimately transform the world according to their visions of the ideal
are the fundamental issues of religious concern.

At the level of man no description of process is
possible without a description of religion. Process
occurs because prehensions of data are given new focus
in new actual occasions, creating novelty and interest.
These prehensions are inseparable from the sensitivities
of emotion and feeling that are experienced at every
unique moment of life. Particularity is the basis for
generality, just as individual moments of experience are
the basis for man, and man is the basis for a civilized
epoch. Thus, religious experiences, which are prehensions of data with a particular nuance or coloration, go
to the very core of process itself.

Whitehead's philosophy, although thoroughly secular, is likewise thoroughly religious. Religion is not simply an activity of man, or even a dimension of his personality. It is a description of the very process of reality at the human level, where sensitivities, feelings and emotions from the world, evoking an appreciation and a reverence for the world, contribute their particularity to process. What is happening in the world because of man takes place because of the religions of man. This is, of course, a very wide sense of religion, but it contains its grain of truth. What a man understands and believes about himself and how he prehends the world are the bases both for his morality and for his liturgy. He acts and celebrates according to the way he has shaped himself, and according to the way he wishes to shape the world. For its part, the world is the richer, or the poorer, because of it.

Whitehead thus inverts the way in which traditional theology understands religion. In the latter, one starts with a proof for the existence of God. Then one argues that man must acknowledge his supremacy. Religion is the way in which man establishes his relationship with God. It includes both the way in which he lives and the manner in which he worships, and it requires that man "practice his religion" both individually and socially. For Whitehead, one starts with religion, not with God. It is because of the experience of the religious along with the secular that one begins to grasp the truth that there is more at issue in the world than the world itself. The reality of God is thus intuited from reality as a whole. Man is thus religious first, and a believer second. Religion is not a consequence of his believing, but a condition for it.

What about God in Whitehead's religion? So far there has been scant mention of God at all. And yet, he has not been far from the discussion. In talking about the world, we have been implicitly talking about God. For the world that man experiences is inseparable from the very nature of God. If man can intuit "extra knowledge" from that world and grasp a certain meaning and depth that go beyond its raw data, this is simply a manifestation of the divine context in which he has found that data. The "something more" that man discovers about his world, and the respect and reverence that this evokes from him, is perhaps the best and only description one can give of the living God this side of speculation.

In one of Whitehead's more often quoted statements, he writes, "The power of God is the worship he inspires."[9] In other words, we are back to liturgy and prayer. What man does with his experiences is the ultimate determinate of the future. The cultivation of religious sensibilities, the sensitivity to the feelings and emotions that arise out of the nature of things, and a reverence and respect for the world as the ultimate source of what can be realized in God is, in the final analysis, the most profound worship that man can hope to offer.

IV

GOD

Nearly a decade has passed since God made the cover of *Time* magazine when it asked rhetorically, "Is God Dead?" Although it did not pretend to give an answer to that question, it did shed much light on a discussion that was being carried on by some of America's leading theologians. Today the subject is just about as dead as God was purported to be. But in its wake we have become much more conscious of how little we can truly say about God, and how careful we must be in saying it.

The "death of God" controversy was not a new phenomenon that suddenly arose in our generation. It was the result of a gradual realization that the way in which we thought and spoke about God was no longer appropriate for expressing those concepts in a particular culture. Indeed, it is an unanswerable question because no human concept or language is ever adequate for divine things. Nevertheless, we must say something about God, because a God about whom we say nothing is a rather useless deity for the religious needs of man.

Even an appeal to the Bible as a source of information about God is not the solution, because the writers of Scripture faced the same problem as secular thinkers when it came to putting on paper the way in which the deity manifested itself to them. They, too, had to resort to human language in the context of a particular human civilization. As a result, the biblical tradition itself raises some problems regarding its representations of God.

On the one hand, we read in the Bible about the Lord who takes sides in history, rewarding the Israelites for their fidelity and punishing their lapses into idolatry. He loves his people, suffers for them, and repeatedly extends to them his mercy and forgiveness. He provides for their needs in the desert, gives them a new land, and defends them from their enemies. He sends prophets to them to remind them of his covenant with them, and despite their hardness of heart, he sends his Son to redeem men from sin and restore them to divine favor. It is a story of God's activity in history, his constant care and concern for his people, and his continual attempts to persuade them to turn from the allurements of the Evil One and to place their trust in his love.

On the other hand, though, the Bible also suggests an image of God as the Eternal One far removed from the petty conflicts of earth. He is Yahweh, "I am who am." His ways are inscrutable, and man has no control over the workings of his divine plan, because he is both unchanging and unchangeable. This side of the biblical God is unseen, unworldly and unknowable. Even his name is shrouded in mystery. Fidelity to him is purely a matter of faith. He is so unrepresentable that alien tribes could ask, "Where is their God?" To those with graven images and large molten idols, the Israelites surely appeared to be the atheists of their time.

Before the early Christian Church could address itself to the problem of finding some theologically acceptable way of representing the biblical God, its rapid movement to the West occasioned its confrontation with a new set of ideas in Greek philosophy. Probably because they were intellectually unimpressed with the myths and deities of their own people, Greek thinkers reasoned to a kind of philosophical deity that was much more a God of eternity than a God of history, much more compatible with the biblical image of Yahweh than with the image of Lord. He was the unmoved mover, the first cause, and an existence unto himself. He was not a God of emotions and feelings, but of transcendence and ultimacy.

The attempt of the Fathers of the Church to reconcile Greek thought with the biblical tradition resulted in the choice of Yahweh over Lord, and this choice has shaped the Christian mind ever since. As a result, God is really not an intrinsic part of history, but one who intervenes from his position in eternity. Time is not real to God, because he knows every event—past, present and future—in a single all-knowing act. Furthermore, he is in his essence devoid of emotions and feelings. He permits evil, even though he does not cause it, and he is not personally engaged in the moment-by-moment struggle against it. He is the complete, self-contained God, fully perfect and without needs. Nothing in the world, or done by the world, can contribute to his intrinsic glory.

Even today much theological opinion prefers the God of philosophy to the God of history. Emotions, feelings and activities are considered accidental to what God is in himself and extrinsic to his divine nature. When applied to God in human discourse, they are simply anthropomorphic representations of him, necessary in order that man have a way of thinking and speaking about the deity. However, these modes of speaking do not tell us anything about the deity itself.

The difficulty is that this very intellectual representation of God never seems quite adequate for religious purposes. Prayer, for example, generally presumes that there is someone who hears and can act upon the merits of a request. God's love for man is not very inspiring when it is stripped of its concreteness and raised to the abstract level of his divine will that all men be saved. The abstract God of the philosopher is not sufficiently consoling to the man of religion. He seeks a more concrete God who can be persuaded, who is personally concerned, and with whom he can talk as one man to another. Christian tradition has always recognized this kind of God, even though Christian thinkers have been loathe to theorize about him. The problem is to find a way to reconcile him with the exigencies of reason.

Is there a way to reconcile the concrete God of religion with the abstract God of philosophy? Can God have feelings and emotions and still be the unchangeable ground of all reality? If he changes, can he still be perfect? Is it possible for him to be a part of the history and structure of reality, and at the same time be the foundation upon which that history and structure are based? Can he be both temporal and eternal, loving and removed, personal and metaphysical, immanent to the world and transcendent of it?

One of the most original and fascinating insights of Whiteheadian philosophy is the way in which it makes this reconciliation. It is a new attempt, born more out of a philosophical need than from a religious concern. And yet, it has captured the imagination of both process philosophers and religious thinkers concerned with the availability of God. Unlike the Scholastic tradition, Whitehead rejects any notion of God as the philosophical ultimate who is self-sufficient and beyond the laws of nature. It is unfortunate, Whitehead maintains, that it was thought necessary to pay him metaphysical compliments. For Whitehead, God is not a last resort who stands outside the system and remains independent of it. Rather, God is an integral element in the whole and participates actively in its struggles and concerns.

The development of Whitehead's idea of God occurred only gradually in his writings. At first he described God merely as the principle of limitation—that principle by which a specific entity does not become other than it is. Here God's function is to envisage the totality of possibility, and to make available to emerging occasions those possibilities that are relevant to its becoming. Limitation is essential to process because some reason must be given for the particularization of what in fact occurs. Without a principle of limitation, there could be no individual, novel actual occasions. In fact, there could be no actual occasions at all.

This position created a philosophical difficulty for Whitehead. If God's function is to envisage possibilities, God has to be real. And the only realities are actual entities. Hence, to bridge the gap between pure possibilities and their real availability to process, God has to be an actual entity in which those possibilities are contained. Therefore, God is that actual entity who gives reality to eternal objects by including them within himself.

Because the ultimates in his system are abstractions from reality and because God is real, Whitehead could not include God in the category of ultimates. God is an actual entity. As an actual entity, he can be described in the same terms as every other actual entity. He is temporal; he prehends physically and conceptually; he has a subjective aim and seeks satisfaction. Furthermore, he is constantly increasing and is an integral part of the process of all reality. Although he is not perfect or ultimate in any absolute sense, he has a perfection and an ultimacy relative to all other things.

In his final statement about God Whitehead developed his theory of divine di-polarity. It is based upon his analysis of an actual entity as prehending both physically and conceptually. God, too, has aspects that allow for physical prehensions and conceptual prehensions. These are called his primordial nature and his consequent nature. The choice of terms is Whitehead's and it may be somewhat confusing for the novice theologian, for we are dealing with a different kind of distinction from what is found in our theological traditions.

In the first place, the words "primordial" and "consequent" have no reference to the antecedent and consequent will of God in Thomistic theology. Thomas' distinction was based upon the necessity for God to restructure the divine plan in the aftermath of man's sin. Whitehead's distinction has to do with the ways in which God is related to other actual entities. Secondly, the term "nature" must not be identified with the divine nature or the human nature of Scholastic theology. In the latter system of thought, nature separates levels of reality according to a hierarchical arrangement—God, angels, man, animals, plants and inanimate matter. For Whitehead, nature is simply an abstract way of talking about how something relates to the rest of reality. Having two natures, therefore, does not imply any real duality since they are merely aspects of the one actual entity.

In other words, the primordial nature and the consequent nature of God are not two individual elements which, as joined together, form the deity. We cannot, at this point, make any meaningful analogies either to the union of the three persons in God (the doctrine of the Trinity) or to the two natures in Christ (the hypostatic union). We are speaking here simply of one God, who is represented as an actual entity and who manifests at least two ways in which his divinity is related to the world.

God's primordial nature, Whitehead says, is independent from his commerce with particulars. It is the abstract side of God, or God "alone with himself."[1] By virtue of his primordiality, God contains within himself the totality of possibility through his conceptual envisagement of the entire multiplicity of eternal objects. In his primordial nature God is without any temporal connotation and without any direction toward individual entities. It is the purely conceptual side of the divinity, without any actuality in itself. Rather, it is the basis of actuality, because it is the foundation for the actualization of possibilities.

As primordial, then, we understand God as the structure of possibility and the context in which actualization takes place. Whitehead uses the terms "ground" and "principle" to illustrate this side of the divinity. It is similar to, but not identical with Paul Tillich's concept of God as "Ground of Being" or the medieval interpretation of "Supreme Being." The difference is that Whitehead is not trying to distinguish the Being of God from other beings, or isolate him into a distinct and unique classification. He is trying to relate God to the whole of reality. Even as primordial, he stresses that God is not *before* all creation, but *with* all creation. God's primordiality is simply a way of talking about how God is related to the world as the context or structure from which all reality emerges.

The images used to describe the primordial nature of God have definite similarities to the God of philosophy and the biblical Yahweh outlined above. It is the impersonal and unknowable side of God, the side not engaged in particulars. In the consequent nature we find the God of history and the Lord of all things. It is the personal aspect of God, whereby he constantly feels what is happening in the world and is affected by the world.

In his consequent nature God is intrinsically related to physical reality. He prehends all of the actual occasions of the physical world as they emerge. Every actual occasion that occurs is thus taken into God and adds its reality to the reality of God. This is why God has a temporal aspect. He is constantly changing as he includes more and more reality in his consequent nature. Indeed, he is constantly *being* changed by that reality. What we do on earth makes a difference to the very reality of God. What we are and how we become affects what God is and how he is to become.

God prehends other actualities in the same way that actual entities prehend each other. There is a physical prehension of the datum according to a particular subjective form. And there are also conceptual prehensions of possibilities in the incorporation of that datum into a new occasion. Because God prehends all actual entities and all eternal objects, every prehension of an actual entity involves both what that actual entity is and what it might have been. In this way God sees the ideal while prehending the actual. Because of his vision, and because of his concern and care for what is happening in reality, he is constantly luring reality on to newer and greater things. Whitehead describes this aspect of God as the "poet of the world, with tender patience leading it by his vision of truth, beauty and goodness."[2]

But God is not an all-powerful, arbitrary ruler of the earth. In fact, he is powerless before the freedom of each individual moment. For in this sense he is no different from every other actual entity. He knows more, because he envisages more. He suffers more, because he knows more. He is, says Whitehead, "the great companion—the fellow sufferer who understands."[3]

One important way in which God is different from other actual entities is that he is an everlasting entity. He does not emerge and perish, only to be succeeded by another occasion, as is the case with the rest of reality. He continues through time as the one enduring reality, prehending all things. As a result, nothing is ever lost, because everything that has ever been is incorporated into the consequent nature of God by virtue of God's prehending it. God is the fullness of all actuality, in whom all actuality is preserved everlastingly. Every actual occasion thus achieves objective immortality in the consequent nature of God and is thus made available as datum for further process in the world.

The consequent nature of God is, therefore, the composite nature of all the actualities of the world, each having obtained its unique representation in the divine nature. We have already seen that each actuality is an organismic unity, whether it be the unity of prehensions in an actual occasion, the unity of a nexus of actual occasions, or even the unity of many nexus. God in his consequent nature is the organism in which all other organisms are prehended and contained. Everything is thus immortalized in the consequent nature of God.

In sum, God is that actual entity that is both the structure or context in which reality emerges (primordial nature) and the totality of that reality (consequent nature). This is because he prehends fully both the totality of possibility (primordial nature) and the totality of actuality (consequent nature). He is both abstract and concrete, eternal and temporal, transcendent and immanent. He can be identified as the God of philosophy as well as the God of history, and he can serve man's metaphysical needs as well as his religious ones. To him we can apply the images both of Yahweh and of Lord.

There is one final thing to say about the God of process philosophy before we can move to the next chapter, where we will consider the implications of God for the world. In several passages of his major work, *Process and Reality*, Whitehead refers to the "superjective nature" of God. It is not entirely clear how this concept fits into his overall schema, but he does describe what he means by the term.

We have just discussed how every actual entity that has ever emerged is taken into God in his consequent nature. God is thus the repository of all reality because he is the unique subject that prehends every actual occasion. But just as this reality contributes to the reality of God, so also is it the data for all further development in the future. In this sense, therefore, God contains the data out of which the world is continuously being renewed. The fact that God contributes what he is in his consequent nature to the on-going process of reality is the meaning of his "superjective nature." This contribution is unique in that God passes back to the world not only the stubborn facts of history, but a sense of what perfected actuality might have been. God can do this because, in addition to prehending the totality of actuality, he also prehends the totality of possibility. In his superjective nature, then, God offers back to the world everything that is of value from the past for the formation of the future.

Is the superjective nature a third nature of God? Considering Whitehead's infrequent reference to it and recalling the number of times he refers only to the primordial and consequent natures, it appears unlikely. It seems instead to be a casual use of the word "nature," perhaps with the specific purpose of warning his readers against employing that word too categorically. The superjective nature might thus best be explained as an aspect of the consequent nature. That is, when considered in its fullest sense, the consequent nature not only gathers into itself all actual occasions that have emerged and perished, but it also makes those occasions available once more to the world in God's own loving way.

This, in brief, is Whitehead's description of God in his philosophical system. It is his way of speaking about the unspeakable. There are many important differences between Whitehead's God and the deity as described in other philosophies. There are even more important differences from the God of religious men. A Christian, for example, may well have some serious reservations about whether this description of God can be harmonized with what he has learned from his tradition.

And yet, despite the difficulties and doubts, there are some significant advantages in Whitehead's explanation. First, he suggests to us a God that comes more from the exigencies of reason than from the psychological needs of man or the uncharted beginnings of his varied traditions. As such, his God is less vulnerable to the attacks of skeptical rationalists. Furthermore, Whitehead's God is concretely alive and active in the world as one who comforts, loves and understands. He is not a candidate for inclusion as an obituary in *Time* magazine. Finally, Whitehead's notion of God does seem to be an adequate way of understanding and explaining the biblical images of God, and perhaps it is even more suitable for this task than the God of Plato or Aristotle, Augustine or Thomas. For the Christian, this may be the most persuasive reason of all.

V

CREATION, GRACE, GLORY AND THE KINGDOM

When first published, Whitehead's reflections about God were favorably received neither by his colleagues in the sciences nor by the religious thinkers who read his works. Scientists, who had come to know him for his careful empirical thinking, were confounded that he considered it important to include God as an essential part of his theoretical system. He seemed thereby to compromise their unspoken professional agnosticism and to mix religious matters with matters of fact. At the same time, he scandalized churchmen because his explanation seemed irreconcilable with their traditional understanding of God, and sometimes it even sounded blasphemous. God was no longer the unmoved mover, the Supreme Being, or the Creator of heaven and earth. There seemed precious little in Whitehead's deity that could, by previous standards, even be recognized as divine.

As Whitehead's thought became better understood among academic theologians and philosophers, it attracted a small but staunch group of followers who found his explanation of God to be both intellectually satisfying and religiously credible. Professor John

Cobb, for example, says that Whitehead's philosophy freed him to speak about God in a way that had been previously impossible for him.[1] Others, too, have been persuaded, but for the most part they are members of the academic community interested in theology or philosophy. Whitehead's insights are only gradually being filtered down for popular understanding and appraisal.

The most persuasive aspect of Whitehead's God from a purely speculative point of view is that he can be integrally related to the world. Rather than the theologically tenuous points of contact between God and the world offered by most other theologies, process thought suggests that God is intimately a part of the world, and that the world is intimately a part of God. Indeed, for Whitehead, God is unthinkable without the world, and the world is unthinkable without God. God, no less than the world, is a relational term, because God must be the God *of* something to be a God at all. God needs a world in order to be God, just as the world needs God in order to be a world. Whitehead's basic insight is that the need of each is completed only in its essential relation to the other.

There are two fundamental relationships between God and the world that every theology must consider. One is the relation of God to the world; the other is the relation of the world to God.

In Thomistic thought, the relation of God to the world is called a *real* relation. This is a technical phrase to describe that the relation constitutes the term of the relationship. That is to say, the term or object of the relation—in this case, the world—could not be what it is except for its relationship to the origin, or subject of the relation, namely, God. There are two ways in which this relation is expressed. In the first, God is related to the world as its creator, without whom the world would not exist. In the second, God is related to his people on earth in the order of grace, or supernatural life.

The first of these is the natural order. God is the Creator of all that exists, and he created all things *ex nihilo* (from nothing). His creatures are of many and differing kinds and species. Among them is man, who is unique in that he is composed of both matter and spirit. Man's body is formed from the dust of the earth, but the soul is created by an individual act of God, at which moment the new human person comes into being. The soul is the spiritual part of man that enables him to be receptive to a sharing in the divine life. The individual creation of the soul and the gift of grace which God offers to it illustrate the second, or supernatural way in which God is related to the world. This relationship is expressed by various concepts in Christian theology, such as grace, divine in-dwelling, participation in the divine life, reconciliation, justification, etc. It is a supernatural relationship because it refers to the disposition of man's soul without affecting what man is in his human nature. By it, the believer is constituted a child of God, as well as God's creature.

The other relationship, that of the world to God, is in Thomistic theory a *rational* relation. This, again, is a technical phrase to designate that the relation only accidentally affects the term of the relation. That is to say, the relation simply adds something extrinsic to the object of the relation, without determining in any way what that object is in itself. In this context Thomistic thought often speaks about God's extrinsic glory. It is the glory that the world gives to God by acknowledging his lordship in worship and obedience. It is distinguished from God's intrinsic glory, which he has eternally in himself as Supreme Being, and to which his creatures can add nothing. At the end of the world the kingdom of God will be established such that God will receive the maximum external glory. The realization of the kingdom will in no way complete God or give him something of which he is in need, for God's intrinsic glory is independent of the status of the kingdom's perfection. God cannot be affected by his creatures except in an extrinsic, accidental way.

A theology based upon Whiteheadian thought differs radically from Thomistic theology in the way in which it describes the concepts of creation, grace, glory and the kingdom. But it can explain them coherently within its own philosophical system. This is what we shall now attempt to do. First, we shall consider the relation in which the two theologies are somewhat alike, that is, the relation of God to the world. This relation includes the concepts of grace and creation.

For Whitehead, as for Thomas, the relation of God to the world is a real, or constitutive relation. God is a formative element in the process or creativity. However, Whitehead rejects the mythical sense of creation in which God is an eternal Being who suddenly starts the time-clocks by an act of creating the material universe, including man. This account of creation, which holds that God created all things *ex nihilo*, does not explain whether or not God was a part of the nothingness out of which creation appeared. Whitehead wishes to avoid the controversy over whether there was before the beginning of things a Creator God who was and still is truly real and omnipotent. He rather affirms categorically that God is a real entity co-extensive in time with the reality of the universe, and that creativity is a way of understanding the whole process of reality, not the beginnings of reality. God, because he is real, corresponds to the categories of all reality by himself being an actual entity. Whether there was a first such entity and how it originated cannot be solved by pushing things back to the beginning, because the beginning of reality is ultimately unexplainable. The only explanation available to us comes from looking at the nature of process as a whole.

Whitehead thus demythologizes the notion of an original act of creation. He describes instead a moment-by-moment emergence of an infinite variety of actual occasions of experience, which he calls "creativity." This process of creativity is, as we have seen, one of the ultimate principles in his scheme of thought. The nature of all reality is that it *becomes*. The concrete actualization of each new occasion takes place when the actual entity of God contributes an initial subjective aim to the convergence of prehensions at the appropriate locus in time and space. Consequently, while it is problematic to say that God creates *ex nihilo*, there is no difficulty in saying that God is like all other actual entities in that he makes a contribution to the concrete emergence of each actual occasion.

There is another way in which God contributes to the world, and that is by offering himself as an actual entity to be prehended. Each emerging actual occasion must take account of God, either positively or negatively, because God is part of the data of its relevant past and the one who makes available all possibility. In prehending God, therefore, the emerging occasion prehends not only the totality of reality as envisaged from its own particular perspective, but also the totality of possibility that is relevant to its own unique becoming. Thus, there is an envisagement of both the real and the possible. This is how God lures the world on to more interesting harmonies and contrasts.

One might argue that in fact God's contribution of an initial aim and his contribution of himself as a datum of prehension are one and the same. Surely they are part of the same general relationship of God to the world. However, an emerging occasion has no freedom regarding its initial aim, which is posited as God's formative contribution to that occasion. It does have freedom regarding the way in which it prehends God; otherwise a divine determination would control everything and God would not be a "fellow sufferer who understands."[2]

If this is correct, then there is a ready parallel to traditional Christian belief. For there are ways in which God's will is final for reality, such as the original act of creation and the individual creation of each man's soul. And there are ways in which God's actions upon us still leave us free, such as our acceptance or rejection of grace.

We can conclude, then, that there is a correspondence between Whitehead's ideas regarding God's relation to the world and the Christian beliefs about creation and grace. Although Whitehead would not posit divine creation as an explanation of the temporal origin of reality, he does ascribe to God a creative function in the emergence of each actual occasion. This function, which is God's giving of an initial aim to each new occasion, is more like the individual creation of each human soul than the single act by which matter was created. This is appropriate, because Whitehead finds the conceptual as well as the physical in every actual occasion and thus assigns an element of spirit and self-determination to each of them.

There is further correspondence in the doctrine of grace and Whitehead's theory of prehensions. Each actual occasion must take account of God by prehending him positively or negatively. In other words, God's grace is always available in each new moment of history. But the free choice of each historical moment or occasion determines to what extent the influence of God will be allowed to enter into the concrete process. How each occasion chooses so as to maximize the importance of divinity for its own becoming constitutes its moral imperative. This will be discussed in more detail in a later chapter.

While the relation of God to the world is similar in both Thomistic theology and process theology in that it is a real relation in both, there is a fundamental difference between the two theologies in explaining the relation of the world to God. For Thomists, as we have seen, this relation is a rational, or accidental relation. For Whiteheadians, it is a real, or constitutive relation.

If it is true to say that God is an integral element in the creative advance of the world by the ways in which he contributes himself to it, it is also true to say that the world contributes itself to the becoming of God. This is because every actual occasion, when it perishes, is added to the consequent nature of God, where it is everlastingly preserved in an objective state. The objectification of past actual occasions in the consequent nature constitutes the sum of God's physical prehensions. Without them, God would not be an actual entity and hence devoid of reality. Because the world contributes what it is physically to the everlasting nature of God, there is a legitimate sense in which we can say that the world makes God real, and without a world, there could be no real God.

Furthermore, when God prehends the world and takes it into himself in his consequent nature, he is thereby changed. As a result, process theology can affirm that what happens in the world does make a difference in God. In this sense, man does "create" his God, as Sigmund Freud and others have suggested. When properly qualified, even the Christian can believe this, because without *something* from the world that redounds back upon God, the world in its totality would have no meaning at all. In Thomistic theology this is God's extrinsic glory. It is the world's contribution to God. But whereas the latter describes this glory as only accidental to what God is in himself, process theology affirms that this contribution changes God and causes his divine becoming. Indeed, process thought maintains that the very reality of God's concrete nature is completely dependent upon what each actual occasion of experience contributes to it. Everything that man does changes what God is essentially, because the relation of the world to God is a *real* relation and is thus constitutive of the term of that relation. God becomes because the world becomes. In Whitehead's paradoxical language, "It is as true to say that God creates the world as that the world creates God."[3]

The addition of each actual occasion in the consequent nature of God means that God must be understood as a multiplicity as well as a single entity. This multiplicity is God in his function as kingdom of heaven. As every actual occasion perishes, it is preserved everlastingly in the consequent nature of God and it is immortalized as part of the kingdom. For God loses nothing that is to be saved. He takes all things up into himself and thereby manifests his kingdom. The kingdom of heaven, then, is already with us, in what God is drawing to himself.

It would be difficult to decide which is the more poetic description of the kingdom—Whitehead's notion of the consequent nature of God or the traditional notion of heaven. There is surely a difference. For Whitehead, the kingdom includes more than merely rational beings. Each moment of creation finds its place in the divine reality, because each occasion manifests a conceptual as well as a physical aspect. Salvation is for all reality, because all reality has value for God and is saved by God. Everything ultimately contributes its own reality to the reality that is God.

This theme is already familiar to many Christians, especially to Catholics, in the writings of Pierre Teilhard de Chardin. For Teilhard, there is a culminative point in process, called the Omega Point, when all that emanated from God in creation returns to God in perfection. For Whitehead, there is no culminative point for the same reason that there is no beginning point. There is a cumulative effect as process continues. The many become one and are increased by one. The kingdom of God is always incomplete and always increasing. Indeed, God himself is incomplete and increasing, because the kingdom is identical with God's own consequent nature. It is not outside of God, to be ultimately reconciled with him, but is rather an aspect of God himself and in constant reconciliation with him. Heaven is not merely seeing God face to face. It is being a part of God and sharing his divine life. The God who gives himself to us in grace is the God to whom we give ourselves in immortality. And just as our acceptance of God enables us to have supernatural life, so God's acceptance of us enables him to have physical life.

Both Teilhard and Whitehead have been criticized on this point for suggesting that ultimately God includes the world in himself. Such a notion treads dan-

gerously near pantheism, which has never been acceptable to Christian faith. Briefly, pantheism is the
doctrine that God is nothing more nor less than the totality of reality, and that only the world deserves our
worship because only it is divine. There is, however, a
great difference between Whitehead's description of
God and the pantheist's description. In the former, God
includes within himself the totality of reality, but he is
not identical to that totality. God is a reality distinct
from the collectivity of all other reality. This notion of
God as including reality and yet being his own reality is
called pan*en*theism. Literally, it means "all *in* God."
Unquestionably, it is a different description of God
from that proposed by traditional theology, but it is not
the same as the pantheism that Christian faith consis-
tently has rejected.

Panentheism is actually a middle position between
the transcendent, immutable God of Scholastic theology and the deification of the world in pantheism. It
posits the individuality and uniqueness of God in a way
that is not possible for pantheism. In Whiteheadian theology, for example, God is a unique, individual entity in
at least two ways. First of all, he is the macrocosmic
unity of all reality. Because in a philosophy of organism
such as Whitehead's, the whole is more than the mere
sum of its parts, the unity of reality is more than the collection of all reality. The macrocosmic unity is itself an
actual entity with its own reality in addition to the totality of reality that constitutes it. In this way, then, God is
at the same time both the totality of reality and the actual entity that is this totality. Secondly, this unique
actual entity, or organism, is the context or structure in
which all the rest of reality becomes, because it includes
both the totality of the past and the totality of possibil-

ity. In this way, too, God is an entity distinct from reality taken as a whole. Hence, the process theologian can talk about God as a real entity in his own right and yet maintain that all things are incorporated into God where they form his kingdom everlastingly.

The process theologian's God, therefore, is both similar to and different from traditional theism and pantheism. It agrees with traditional theism and differs from pantheism in maintaining God's individuality—that he is more than the structure and totality of the cosmos and that he is in one sense distinct from it. It agrees with pantheism and differs from traditional theism in maintaining God's immanence to the world—that he is in all reality and that all reality is in him. In this sense reality is identifiable with the deity, for God's reality cannot be less or other than all-inclusive of the structure and totality of reality in the cosmos. This is the middle way of panentheism. It is a way never formally considered by the Christian faith, and its ultimate acceptance or rejection will be determined only by whether it can persuade Christians that it is a more suitable explanation of what they believe about God than the traditional explanations.

The chief advantage of panentheism over traditional theism is that it more adequately describes the divine immanence in the world without compromising the divine transcendence. The latter is manifest in the fact that God is a unique actual entity, different from any other entity that has existed or can exist. And yet the function of that entity—indeed that which makes him unique—is to be immanent to the world and to take the world immanently into himself. This is the result of describing the relations of God to the world and the world to God as both being real relations. God is comprehensible only because of the world, and the world is comprehensible only because of God.

Traditional theology has always been faced with a certain ambiguity on this issue. On the one hand, God is seen as transcendent, other-worldly, and self-sufficient. He is essentially an outsider who created all things in the beginning and occasionally reaches back into the world in order to influence the process of events by his grace. But that process in no way influences the eternal Being of God. To the extent that traditional theology speaks about God in himself, he is transcendent; to the extent that it speaks about God's grace, he is immanent. But how the transcendent God bridges the gap to become immanent, and why his grace touches some events and not others, are left to the realm of mystery.

Process theology, on the contrary, provides the believer with a God who is equally immanent and transcendent. In fact, given the process philosophical perspective, the difficulty does not even arise. God is really in the world, an integral part of its process. He touches each actual entity, not from the outside, but from within the process itself. He is constantly contributing himself to the whole of reality through the prehensive activity of all other actual entities. Each moment becomes what it is because of God's contribution both of an initial aim and of himself as datum for the emergence of the new occasion. God touches all things because he is really a part of all things. He is his own self, and thus transcendent, but he is also within and indeed woven into the very tissue of each actual occasion in a most intimate way.

At the same time all things are immanent to God and touch him in his consequent nature. They touch

God immanently because they are really a part of God as constitutive elements of that nature. Immanence, therefore, is a mutual relationship between God and the world. Indeed, mutuality is the condition for a genuine immanence. This is why process theology holds that the relations both of God to the world and the world to God are real relations, and why it rejects the Scholastic notion that there can be a rational, or accidental relation of the world to God.

VI

MAN

Besides being the age of science, the twentieth century has also been the age of man. Volumes have been written interpreting the human phenomenon from a variety of perspectives. In fact, entire sciences, such as anthropology, sociology, and psychology, have been developed into scholarly curricula for study and investigation at universities around the world. Some of the newly developed theories tend to support what Christians have traditionally believed about man, while others have challenged those beliefs. As a result, Christians have had to rethink and reformulate their opinions about the nature of man, while endeavoring to keep within the general tradition of their faith.

Process thought has its own interpretation of what man is. It differs in important ways from the traditional understanding of man, as well as from some of the more important new theories, such as existentialism and behaviorism. It is a philosophical interpretation, formulated in the difficult process terminology with which we have already become somewhat familiar. It is important to us not only because of its insights about man, but also because of its contributions to Christology, morality and immortality, which will be the subjects of later chapters.

As one might suspect from the preceding chapters, the human person is a very complex concept in Whiteheadian thought, raising many new and interesting questions never confronted by traditional philosophy. Man, like all other realities, is described in terms of actual occasions, not in terms of a single underlying substance. These actual occasions are in a serial order, so that the history of an individual man is traced out and defined by their continuity or historical route through time. What traditional philosophy called the individual substance of a man is called an enduring object in process philosophy in order to remind us of its composite and temporal nature. However, an enduring object is an abstraction from reality, and not the reality itself, which is the series of actual occasions.

Man is not the only kind of enduring object. Buildings, trees and planets also are series of actual occasions in historical patterns. The difference is that in man and the higher animals there is a unique coordination of many such occasions over a particular area called the body, and a unique inheritance of past occasions that is able consciously to identify a self through history. These coordinating occasions constitute the personal living nexus of occasions by which a person is defined. There is, consequently, a basis for speaking about a body and a soul in Whiteheadian philosophy. It is, however, a very different kind of body and soul than is explained in traditional Christian doctrine. The distinction in process thought is not between the two component elements of matter and spirit conjoined to form a person, but between high-grade, or coordinating occasions, and low-grade occasions in a living nexus, each of which is its own reality.

Whitehead formulates his description of man on

the basis of how we experience ourselves. For example, a man experiences his body as himself, and yet the self is also experienced as distinguishable from any particular part of the body. This explains why the "self" is not divided when one part of the body is severed from the rest. It also explains why experience always occurs through the mediation of the body. Actually, what a man experiences is a complex unity of happenings within a certain field that he identifies as the self. This complex unity is the coordinated functioning of the billions of cells that compose his body, thus suggesting that the body is a coordinated nexus of actual occasions in space and time. Many of these occasions also interact in specialized ways with each other, providing the internal functioning and the sense awareness of a living organism. They are all unified by a central occasion, probably located in the brain, by which the body considers itself one experiencing subject. This central occasion coordinates the various secondary centers which themselves coordinate and transmit what is happening in the various specialized functions of the body.

The actual occasions that constitute the body are truly identifiable with the self, but less so than is the central, or coordinating occasion by which the self is an experiencing subject. Nevertheless, the central occasion is never independent of the lower-grade occasions of the body, for it depends upon these for its data, its mood, and its every contact with the world outside. Beyond the body there are also occasions which are closely related to the central occasion, but which are not directly part of the body that it coordinates. These are mediated to the central occasion by the other occasions of the body. Ordinarily, this distinction between bodily occasions is easily made by the central occasion, or experiencing subject. For example, although I can speak of the instrument with which I am writing as *my* pen, I am intuitively aware that it is not a part of me in the same way in which *my* fingernails are. When we consider food or breath, however, the distinction is not as clear. At what point does a molecule of oxygen or a carbohydrate cease being what it is and begin to function as part of the body? The same problem exists in the psychological order when we try to define when an external event becomes an internalized emotion of the person. These examples simply illustrate the fact that the outer limits of the self cannot always be precisely established. Just as the self, or soul, seems to blend into the body, so too the body seems to blend into its immediate environment. Man is a difficult reality to isolate and define.

The body, therefore, is not principally that which identifies the self. It is that which links the self to the rest of reality. Or, to put it another way, the body is the way in which man is located in the world and made a part of it. Whitehead's point is simply that there is a continuity of relationships from the central occasion that defines the self to the many remote occasions which the self cannot prehend. My body and my world are merely steps in these relationships by which all things are related in a total unity of reality.

The self, or coordinating occasion, is what corresponds most closely to the Christian concept of soul. Whitehead himself uses the term, but not with its religious connotation. He describes it vaguely as the life, or the mind of certain enduring objects; in man it is the experience of his own uniqueness.

The chief difference from traditional Christian thought is that Whitehead's soul is not a substantial

form that endures through time and into eternity. It is
rather the succession of coordinating occasions that define the self. Whitehead refers to the soul as the "coordinated stream of personal experiences," and as "the
thread of life."[1] Clearly, these images are not in-
terchangeable with those found in the Christian tradition. A second important difference from the tradition
is that this soul does not distinguish man from other
forms of creation because the soul is found in the more
complex animals as well as in man. It exists in any enduring object where there is a single center of experience that coordinates the functioning of the organism
as a whole. Having a soul is thus a matter of degree.
Higher organisms have a higher-grade soul than lower
organisms because they are constituted by a series of
higher-grade actual occasions. Presumably, even among
men there is a difference in soul. It is thus not a question of having a soul or not. As Whitehead puts the
question, it is, "How much, if any?"[2]

If the soul is a series of actual occasions in a coordinating role vis-à-vis the total organism, how can it account for a man's identity through time? The implications of this question are very important, because if
there is no way of making such an accounting, then
there is no way that a man's past actions can be imputed to his present self. Without the same person enduring through time, there is no logical basis for accountability for the past or responsibility for what has been
done.

The common assumption of every civilization is
that such an accountability for the past can and ought
to be made. This assumption is based on the premise
that we are in fact the same person we were yesterday
and even last year, despite the interval of time and the

variety of new experiences that have intervened. And yet, change and the freedom to change also are generally assumed. The old man is no longer the child. He has changed both physically and psychically. In addition, there are moments in which a person may choose to reorient his life, sometimes in a very fundamental way. This kind of change is the basis for a metanoia, or conversion, whereby a person renounces the direction his life took in the past and determines on a new course of action. These changes, too, are changes in the self, and they likewise must be accounted for in any description of man's soul. Therefore, a philosophy of man must be able to explain both the freedom of the present moment and the responsibility for the past if it wishes to be in accord with what civilizations generally presume.

The process philosopher has less difficulty in accounting for changes in the soul than he does in explaining its continuity. Change occurs as each occasion becomes its own unique synthesis of its past and its relevant environment. At every moment some change takes place, because every moment is a new synthesis. At some moments the change is great enough to be perceptible to the self and perhaps even to others. Such a moment occurs when a particular experience triggers a reorientation of relevant data and causes a metanoia. At any particular moment or occasion of its series, the soul is free to do this, because no occasion is fully determined in its own synthesis by the occasions that preceded it. Hence, there is always the freedom to initiate novelty and bring about a conversion.

Even after such a conversion, one still experiences himself in a continuity with his past, albeit a redirected past. How can this very strong sense of oneness over time be described in process terminology?

The basic continuity of the human soul through time—indeed the continuity of any enduring object through time—is the result of a continuous prehending of its own enduring past. A prehension, we must remember, is not merely an extrinsic influence of one entity upon another. It is the incorporation or inclusion of the former entity in the latter. The former is, therefore, an ultimately real feature of the latter, and thus is a real continuity of the enduring object through time. In addition, the environment within which the new occasion emerges is not that much different from the way its predecessor synthesized that reality. Change is always possible, and in fact is always occurring, at least in small ways, but radical change is the exception and ought never to be presumed.

Prehensions, therefore, explain the relation between one actual entity and its immediate predecessor in a series, and this relation is so intimate that the successive occasions do form, in reality, one enduring object. We might use the model of human memory to illustrate the relation, although it is not adequate as an explanation. When a person remembers something that took place in the past, that past event is re-presented, or made present once again. There is a return of the past to the present in a picture or concept which represents that past event. In this way the past is rendered immanent to the present by means of what is remembered. The weakness of this illustration in describing Whitehead's theory of prehensions is that in memory only pictures or concepts are brought into the present. In prehensive activity, the experience itself is re-presented, and that experience is the reality. The past is immanently incorporated into the present, and becomes part of the present. There is a "peculiar completeness"[3] in each present moment that can only be explained in terms of its inclusion of the past. Because the present is the peculiar completeness of the past, it identifies itself with its past. Thus, in a personal series of actual occasions the present actual occasion can be imputed with responsibility for the past in a limited way.

Imputing responsibility has always posed a problem for civilized man. On the one hand, some degree of responsibility for one's personal past has been almost universally presumed. In some civilizations, responsibility has also been extended to one's ancestoral past, so that the wrongs of the parents or grandparents could also properly be attributed to the offspring. On the other hand, however, many civilizations, especially the more liberal ones of the present epoch, have been painstakingly careful to acknowledge the possibility of a personal change of heart and to enable the person to escape the more painful consequences of his own past behavior provided he is genuinely repentant.

The Whiteheadian perspective seems quite adequate to deal with this dilemma. It acknowledges that a person's inheritance does have a causal influence over him, and that in a very minimal degree he may appropriately take on certain responsibilities from his ancestors and enjoy certain kinds of inheritances from them, because he is really related to them. A person is much more responsible for his own past actions, because they are a part of the direct personal series of occasions that constitute the self. If a wrong has been committed, he is held responsible for its commission and for restitution, if necessary. And yet, as in Christian belief, there is a possibility for metanoia and forgiveness, and a person who has genuinely repented for his past need not be permanently treated as a transgressor, because in one sense he is different from the person he was formerly.

The problem is to identify genuine repentance. And here again Whiteheadian philosophy follows closely the common human experience. There is in each new occasion always some change from the previous occasion in that series. However, because its primary prehension is of its own preceding occasion and because its other prehensive activity is of an environment greatly similar to its predecessor, the possibility for radical change is slight. The factors that were contributory to the preceding occasions are, for the most part, still in existence and reinforcing of a continuance of a similar occasion. Therefore, applied to the person, there is always a possibility that a genuine repentance and metanoia can occur, but the presumption is always against any fundamental change. Hence, genuine conversion—the condition for a mitigation of responsibility —must be demonstrably present before it can be assumed. This is true regardless of the quality that might be attributed to the behavior. The immanence of the past on the present and its inclusion in the emerging occasion is just as operative for evil as for good.

With respect to human freedom and responsibility, the interpretation of man in process thought is very compatible with the presumptions of Christian faith. Man is free to construct what he will become from the data available to him. Granted, he is not free with respect to the composition of that data, but he is free regarding what he does with it. He is also responsible, for what he chooses to do will provide the data for the future. Furthermore, he will be held accountable for that choice in his own personal future because his decision will be immediately included in and determinative of what he will be in the future. For the future self is in direct succession with the present self. He will not, of course, be exactly the same person, and consequently he will feel less responsibility for the past than he will feel for maximizing the present moment's contribution to the future. But, in the absence of a fundamental re-evaluation of the past in a moment of genuine meta-noia, he will remain accountable to himself for that past in all of its ramifications, since it will continue to live on in him. In this way, man continues to experience a freedom with respect to the present and a responsibility with respect to the past and the future. This position corresponds to Christian belief as well as to the practices of most civilizations.

In conclusion, can we say that the explanations of process theology are generally compatible with Christian beliefs regarding body and soul? This is a more formidable task than can be properly undertaken here. Let it suffice to note that the traditional body-soul distinction generally associated with Christian belief is more a Hellenic distinction than a biblical one. The Scriptures do speak of the body, but more as a living entity than a material one. And they do speak of the spirit, or breath, which symbolizes the life of the body. The Greek distinction between matter and form, technically called the hylomorphic theory, seemed for ages of Christians an adequate way of speaking about man and explaining the basic insight of the Bible. This distinction is the basis for the theory that man is a composite of matter (called the body) and an informing principle of life (called the soul). But this explanation does not exclude the possibility of other distinctions which also shed light upon the biblical revelation about man and which may give rise to other theories, such as the White-headian one we have described.

In an age when our experience of change and process is more fundamental than our experience of a static or stable matter and form, some theory other than that of the Greeks may prove to be more helpful for developing a contemporary understanding of man. In other words, it may be necessary to reformulate our interpretation of the Scriptures from the hylomorphic concepts to more expansive, evolutionary concepts, in order to correspond better to our fundamental experience of a changing man in a changing reality.

VII

JESUS

A recent survey revealed that among clergymen today the most perplexing theological question is: "What can we say about Jesus Christ?" It is an old question, one that dates back to Jesus' own interrogation of his disciples. Curiously, it is being reasked by Christian clergymen at a time when so many others are unhesitatingly becoming part of the Jesus movement or returning to fundamentalist churches. Interest in the person of Jesus has perhaps never been greater, and the spectrum of opinion as to who he is and what he means to modern man has never been wider.

For the clergyman, the question of Jesus is not generally a crisis of faith or a skepticism about the world of Christianity or its message. It is rather the result of coming to grips with much new scholarship regarding both the biblical origins of the faith and new interpretations of tradition. From biblical scholarship alone, for example, we probably know more today about the life and times of Jesus than was known at any period since the second generation of Christians. Archeological explorations of the Holy Land and surrounding areas have given some important insights about the people of that period and their ways of thinking and writing. New insights into the language used by Jesus and the languages in which the Gospels were originally written have also added to a better understanding of the Christian message. In addition, advances in secular philosophy and literary criticism have enabled scholars to be much more accurate in the way in which they interpret the Gospels and other religious writings. Hermeneutics has become an important science in its own right.

At the same time there has been at the other extreme almost an unquestioning and uncritical acceptance of Jesus by many other Christians, especially among large groups of young people without any formal church affiliation. They accept Jesus literally as their personal Lord and Savior and do not in practice make a distinction between him and God. The Bible, the prayer meetings, and the witness of their fellow believers provide them with the support and direction they need in their lives. In some cases the commitment is so intense as to include an abandoning of their former life-style. For most of them, biblical scholarship and hermeneutics are not important. Jesus reveals his will to them through the readings of the Scriptures and in prayer, and doing his will is all that really matters. Intellectual distinctions and interpretations of doctrine are merely a curiosity of the rationalist, and not usually conducive to witnessing the faith. This neo-fundamentalism has been on the increase in recent years despite—or perhaps because of—all the new and complex scholarly information now available about the historical person of Jesus. It has created an ever-widening chasm between the new believer and the careful student of the Bible, among whom are many so-called "liberal" or "relevant" clergymen.

The problem is to reconcile the Jesus of the scholars with the Jesus of the believers in a way that genuinely profits from contemporary scholarship without compromising the credibility of Jesus as Lord and Savior. In other words, what can we say about Jesus that is faithful both to the historical Jesus and to the belief of his followers? It is fundamentally a question of finding a language suitable for describing the person of Jesus and his significance for today.

The problem of finding suitable language is not a new one in the history of Christianity. It first emerged shortly after the foundations of Christianity itself in a form very similar to today's. The problem at that time was how to reconcile the humanity of Jesus with his followers' profession of his divinity. It was not an easy problem to resolve, and it was immensely complicated by the fact that when the disciples of Jesus began preaching his message, they took the message westward, where they immediately encountered Greek philosophical thought. Thus, even before Christianity had a chance to define itself in terms of its own Hebrew origins, it was already being called upon to deal with an alien culture which had a level of philosophical sophistication higher than its own. The primitive faith in Jesus therefore had to be expressed accurately within the thought patterns of a second culture before it had the opportunity to mature adequately in its original culture.

The Hebrew understanding of Jesus is best represented by the Gospels and the non-Pauline epistles. It is filled with concrete images, models and stories, all characteristic of Hebrew literature. The title "Son of God" is an example. When we consider that the creedal formulation of the Trinity had probably not yet been conceived, we become aware that this title had quite a different connotation to the early Hebrew Christian, for whom it meant "privileged creature of God," than it had to the later Greek Christian, who transposed it to the form "God the Son," meaning the second person of the Trinity. The pre-Hellenic language about Jesus was not a denial of the divinity in him, but the use of a different, more mythical literary form. It was intended to affirm that the Hebrew believers did experience God at work in Jesus, and that in him they experienced the revelation of God's own love. In this way it was quite different from Greek language which preferred a more philosophical literary form to interpret Jesus' relation to God. Thus the Greek implication of metaphysical plurality in God as a result of the divinity of Jesus was a foreign idea to the Jews because of their strict monotheistic heritage.

For the Greeks, reconciling the divinity and the humanity in the single person of Jesus was not as impossible as it seemed for the Hebrews. Theirs was a polytheistic tradition, and plurality in God was not an insurmountable difficulty. What was essential to them, however, was to incorporate Jesus into the divinity in such a way as to raise him beyond the petty gods and goddesses of their tradition. Thus the affirmation of a single deity containing three persons, the second of whom was the eternal person of "God the Son," was a clear and consistent theological explanation of the divinity of Jesus in the framework of their philosophy. This explanation, which seemed to express adequately the experience of the early Christians, has continued ever since to function as the authentic expression of the faith.

This Hellenic formulation of the Trinity in the creeds and the definitions of the Christological dogmas at Nicaea, Ephesus, and Chalcedon became the normative statements of Christian belief about Jesus. In other words, the criteria for determining orthodoxy shifted from the original experience of Jesus to statements about what that experience meant. And these normative statements were formulated in a particular philosophical frame of reference, phrased in its terminology, illustrated by its distinctions, and encased in its limitations.

In view of the fact that our knowledge of Jesus and his times is superior even to the knowledge of those early councils or creedal authors, there is a growing dissatisfaction with continuing to employ the traditional statements as theological norms. This is in no way a denial of the fact that these norms did serve as adequate expressions of the Christian faith for centuries of believers. But with the knowledge presently available to theology and with the vast change of philosophical perspective that has occurred since the first centuries of Christendom, tentative new formulations of the original Christian experience that are not always literally contained within the traditional normative statements are now being proposed by theologians from a variety of philosophical perspectives. Process theologians are among those making such tentative formulations.

Truly this work is tenuous, insofar as it depends a great deal upon both the findings of biblical scholars and a creative understanding of the tradition that it seeks to interpret. Furthermore, it must be carried on in dialogue among the biblical exegete, the historical theologian, and the contemporary interpreter. Each must refine and enrich the perspective of the others. Such a task is obviously beyond the scope of any one person or book. In this introduction to process thought, we can only hope to sketch out a possible understand-

ing of the person of Jesus and his significance to our
contemporary world based upon a very general familiarity with advances being made in biblical and her-
meneutical studies. What we are doing, however, is very
similar to what the Christians of the first few centuries
did. We are attempting to explain the primitive Christian experience of Jesus in the language of a philosophical perspective of God and man to suggest how that
perspective might deal with the inter-relation of humanity and divinity in the person of Jesus, who is called the
Christ.

Essentially, the primitive Christian experience is
that Jesus claimed a unique relationship with God, and
that his disciples experienced God at work in and
through him. Furthermore, they accepted his teachings
as ultimately normative for their own lives and for the
world. In other words, in the person of Jesus the first
disciples experienced God manifested to them in a
unique and decisive way. Process theology is one attempt to offer a new, tentative explanation in modern
terminology of how God was uniquely present in the
person of Jesus and how that presence is still decisive
for us today.

As an historical person, Jesus was human in exactly the same way we are human. The description of the
humanity of Jesus, therefore, is the same as it is for
every man. He was composed of body and soul, that is,
of nexūs of low-grade occasions coordinated by an ordered series of high-grade occasions, which traced his
personal identity through his own life-history. Each
moment of that personal history was its own unique occasion, arising out of the series with its own particular
initial aim, prehending the past of that series and the relevant environment, and freely arriving at its own syn-

thesis before ceding its reality to the new occasion emerging from it. This philosophical pattern is the basis for explaining how it is possible for one man, namely Jesus, to have enjoyed a unique relationship with God, and how the consequences of that relationship are still important to us.

There are two ways in which we can argue that Jesus was a unique person. The first concerns the sequence of initial aims in the soul of Jesus; the second deals with the manner in which he prehended. We must remember that the source of every initial aim for each actual occasion is God himself. The convergence of the past into a new locus in space and time can be realized as a new actual occasion only when God contributes an initial aim. Therefore, God contributed the initial aim to each successive moment of Jesus' life.

This alone might be sufficient theological basis for describing the divinity of Jesus. One can simply maintain that in Jesus the initial aim that God contributed was at each and every moment to be his Son, or, in more philosophical language, to realize the divinity at every occasion in the series. Jesus, responding to the promptings of these initial aims, freely chose to realize that divinity by directing the synthesis of each and every occasion of his life toward the fulfillment of that divine initiative. Every moment of his life was an acceptance and a reaffirmation of God's special initiative on his behalf. In religious language, every moment was a moment of grace; he was like us in all things but sin.

There is, however, a certain difficulty that some process theologians find with the above explanation. It is the positing of an arbitrary initiative on the part of God that applied solely to the person of Jesus. Such an arbitrariness still makes Jesus a somewhat artificial insertion into history. This raises the impossible question: Why only in Jesus? If God's initial aim is totally free and arbitrary, why does he not call all of us to such a divine relationship with him by virtue of his universal love? One can, of course, simply consign the inquiry to the realm of mystery, but the theologian by profession must remain unsatisfied until he can be assured that there is no better way of dealing with the problem.

Perhaps indeed God would offer to each occasion an initial aim to realize the divinity, but because of inherent limitations that even God cannot circumvent, such an aim can only be expressed partially in most occasions. For example, the nature of the sequence of occasions that characterizes a stone does not allow for consciousness, simply because that mode of prehending is not available to an occasion in that series. God's initial aim for such an occasion is consequently limited by the kinds of prehensions available in that nexus. In other words, in giving an initial aim, God himself is limited to the kinds of determinants out of which that occasion is emerging.

When God contributes an initial aim to a high-grade occasion in a personal series, he is likewise limited by the prior environmental factors that have been shaping that series, especially by the past occasions in the series itself. There is always a call to fuller realization of the divinity in each occasion, but for most occasions that realization cannot achieve the unlimited fullness that it achieved in Jesus. Thus, due to cultural, familial and other environmental conditions, God was able to initiate the possibility of a full relationship with the person of Jesus from the beginning, and at every moment of his life Jesus freely chose to affirm and maximize the initiative that was his.

This latter explanation is more involved than the former, but it has the advantage of avoiding any arbitrariness on the part of God. Thus, it escapes the mythological pitfalls that beset explanations in which some human events can be described only in terms of special and distinctive interventions of God. A theological system in which God acts exactly the same way toward every occasion avoids the necessity of justifying certain divine actions or explaining the absence of others.

There is a second element in process thought that provides a further possibility to describe the uniqueness of the person of Jesus. This is the theory of prehensions. Each actual occasion is the result of many prehensions that are synthesized into one coherent whole. These prehensions are the relations of the occasion to its own past and to its relevant environment. One such prehension is necessarily the prehension of the divinity. It can focus upon that prehension and make it a significant component in its synthesis, or it can render it trivial. On most occasions, the prehension of the divinity is not significant in the final synthesis, but on some occasions, such as moments of prayer or spiritual enlightenment, it can be the dominant element.

To say that Jesus prehended the divinity in an intense way would imply that he maintained a stronger relation with God than is common to most men. It would not in itself, however, make him unique, because the same kind of explanation would describe the prophet or mystic. Nor can we say that Jesus prehended only the divinity, because this would place his humanity into question. Rather, we might suggest that Jesus prehended God at every moment of his life in such a way that his relation to God partially displaced his experience of self, so that in fact Jesus could have experienced himself as both human and divine. That is to say, the series of actual occasions that defined the person of Jesus were marked by prehensions of the deity according to the same mode that marked his prehensions of his own human past. Therefore, the self that Jesus experienced throughout his life was a moment by moment integration of the human and divine in his own person.

This is, of course, the maximal statement a process theologian can make about Jesus. Translated back into the traditional terminology of two natures in one person, it seems to conform quite adequately to what was proclaimed at Ephesus and Chalcedon. It is a clear reaffirmation of the divinity of Jesus and a strong basis for acknowledging him as Lord and Master, as do the Jesus movement and other fundamentalist groups today. At the same time, for the so-called liberal Christians to whom this may seem too much like philosophical mythology, the explanation of Jesus as simply a holy man with intense prehensions of the deity provides the description of a fully human person who was related to God in a very special way.

Thus, Jesus is unique either in the unique composition that he experienced as his "self" or in the fact that no other person has ever achieved such a total relation with God. Either way, process theology can accommodate the Christian seeking a philosophical explanation of the person of Jesus. This is a distinct advantage, because it enables process theology to reduce the differences among Christians to the way in which prehensions of the divinity can be posited in the person of Jesus.

When we consider both the initial aim and the prehensions of God by Jesus as factors in resolving the question of reconciling the humanity and divinity in

Jesus, we must understand that the basis of the process explanation is the theory of immanence, namely, the divine immanence in Jesus. God is immanent to every actual occasion both in giving it its initial aim and in that occasion's own prehensions of the deity. Jesus is unique because the immanence of God finds expression in him in a unique way. This is why his followers were amazed that he spoke with his own authority. With God's immanence totally present to him at all times, Jesus did not need to appeal to the tradition or even to some private revelation. He spoke from the depths of the divinity that was in him, and in this way he persuaded his hearers both by what he was and by what he said.

What is decisive in Jesus and what makes him significant for all subsequent history is that in his person God reveals himself to us as immanent in our world. He is not merely the prime mover of Greek philosophy or the God of the covenant in the Old Testament. He is, as Augustine so succinctly stated, more intimate than I am to myself. God's immanent presence to every man is made known in his presence in Jesus. This is the significance of the incarnation. God is immanently present in Jesus and in our world. Conversely, the significance of the death and resurrection is that Jesus is immanently present in God. God has taken what is human and worldly into himself in a complete and positive way. Man and his world are not alien to God or insignificant to him. We are indeed, moment by moment, likewise being taken up into the divine nature and "resurrected" into objective immortality where we become part of the prehendable data for future occasions. Great, admirable men of history, such as Socrates, Buddha and St. Francis, are examples of persons whose lives and inspirations are continually being resurrected from the past for the edification of emerging moments of history. In Jesus this resurrection was uniquely striking, because it was experienced by his followers immediately after his death, and it has continued to be a part of the Christian faith experience ever since.

The purpose of Jesus in history, therefore, and his continued significance for us today, is his redemptive function. The term "redemption" is perhaps somewhat misleading in this context. Literally, it means "buying back." In the tradition of Irenaeus, Anselm and Thomas, this referred to God's act in Jesus of buying us back from the consequences of original sin. Process theologians generally prefer the tradition of John Duns Scotus, which holds that God predestined the person of Jesus as the crowning of creation and as the total manifestation of his love, regardless of whether man sinned. In process theology Jesus is the primordial example of God's immanence in the world and the world's immanence in God. Redemption, consequently, states the fact that man need not slavishly move through life from occasion to occasion, merely creating each new synthesis from worldly data in pursuit of worldly satisfaction, but that he is freed to respond to the divine immanence within him and within the world, thus constantly striving, occasion by occasion, to maximize a realization of that divinity as best he can, within the limitations imposed by his history and his environment. In brief, redemption is the freedom to appeal to the immanent divinity in the self as a more perfect authority than the authority of history or environment alone.

We have not answered definitively the question of whether Jesus is an absolutely unique person and absolutely decisive for human history, or whether he is merely the primordial model of human existence. Is he different in kind, or only in quality? There are, as we have seen, ways in which process philosophy can be used to argue both positions. Christian tradition, until relatively recently, has been very careful to insist upon an absolute distinction between the person of Jesus and other human persons. Is this absolute a part of the original Christian experience, or is it rather the result of the Hellenic concept of God that underlay the Christological dogmas? To put the question in another way, is it necessary to hold Jesus' absolute distinctiveness as divine if one's philosophy does not hold God's absolute distinctiveness from the world? Is it not accurate to say that the divinity of Jesus is represented more by the way in which he was really related to God than by the way in which he was unrelated to the world? And if his relation to God constitutes the ideal relation for every man (even though it may be impossible to realize this ideal in every successive occasion the way it was realized in Jesus), can we not say that what best characterizes the divinity of Jesus is precisely that he was ideally human?

This line of reasoning can put aside the old notion that uniqueness requires an absolute distinction from all other reality. Instead, it suggests that uniqueness can be a relative term, and that Jesus is in fact unique because in his humanity he is a more perfect model of ideal humanity than has ever existed, or, we may believe, will ever exist in the future. Since man is most ideally human when he responds to the immanence of God in every occasion of his continuity, both by the realization of God's initial aim and by his positively prehending God, Jesus is most divine when he is most ideally human. He is divine not because of an absolute

difference from other men, but because of the realization of divinity within him. For divinity does not
require such a difference; indeed it denies such a difference, since the God who is immanent in Jesus is the
God in whose consequent nature the world is immanent. The very nature of God in process theology
rejects such an absolute distinction between Jesus and
the rest of humanity, except as an abstract mode of
speaking.

Jesus is really related to God, and really related to
man, just as God is really related to man. The mode of
Jesus' relation to God, however, is such that God is experienced as uniquely present in him. This relation,
which constitutes his divinity, in no way renders him
different from us, but more an intimate part of us. He
is divine because he is the primordial exemplification of
God's immanence in the world, and our ultimate immanence in God. In him we are freed to discover the
divinity in each new occasion of life. Jesus is thus the
primordial model of human life lived in freedom and
love. In him man can find both his meaning and his
Savior.

VIII

THE CHURCH

Institutions are not having a very happy time of it these days, and the Church, despite its long and venerable tradition, is no exception. Like the other parts of the so-called "establishment," the Church is now suspect of being inflexible and unresponsive to the needs of a rapidly changing twentieth century. Furthermore, since its ultimate claim to existence is rooted more in the events of the past than in contemporary social problems, it has even a more conservative image than political and economic institutions. As a result, many today have abandoned their ties to organized Christian churches and replaced them with more personal forms of religious beliefs.[1]

A Christian church that is not in some way related to human concerns has lost the spirit of its foundation in Jesus and has little to recommend it to the world at large. Mindful of this fact, Pope John XXIII convoked the Second Vatican Council for the purpose of making necessary reforms in the Roman Catholic Church. The history of the Council is now well known, and its repercussions have been felt by Catholics and non-Catholics alike. Its spirit continues in the Church into our own time, even though the old concerns have given way to new ones. Because it focused internally upon reform

and adaptation, and externally upon dialogue and interaction with other churches, its thrust can best be
described as forward and outward. Fidelity to the
Council thus implies not merely a repetition of its formulae or even a restudying of its documents. We are no
longer afforded the luxury of looking backward for security and stability. There is no longer any reprieve
from the task of continuing to build the Church of the
future. The Vatican II Catholic, therefore, is one who is
willing to think beyond the Council and to engage in
the creative process that ought to characterize the
Church.

The key to understanding Vatican II can perhaps
best be expressed in two phrases that characterized it.
They are the description of the Church as *semper reformanda* (always in need of reform) and as *populi Dei*
(the people of God). These expressions characterize a
new self-image of the Church that began to emerge at
the Council. They suggest a replacement of the old
model of the Church as a monolithic, unchanging institution to a new model that uses evolutionary and relational modes of thought.

The old model of the Church was a faithful reflection of the old substance mode of philosophy that had
characterized the Church since the fourth century. It
was a stable, definable institution established by Jesus
and transmitted in its total essence throughout the ages.
It was infallible and indefectible, and change affected it
only accidently. Those who could acknowledge in faith
its claim to possessing the eternal truths could become
members of the institution by baptism. In a certain
sense, however, the Church was self-sufficient by virtue
of its divine foundation, and even its members were ex-
traneous to its essential nature and structure. It was,

Catholics were taught, a "perfect society," i.e., complete unto itself in its purposes and the adequate means of attaining them.

The two expressions referred to above suggest that the mode[1] of the Church has changed considerably since Vatican II. The new model has not yet been fully formulated either theoretically or operationally. But the spirit of the Council and the events in the Church subsequent to it suggest that the new model is heavily imbued with processive and organismic patterns of thought.

The processive nature of the Church is implied in the expression *Ecclesia semper reformanda.* In its origin, the Church was the society that developed when followers of Jesus made an act of faith in him. Its continued existence has depended upon others reiterating that act of faith in Jesus throughout its entire history. Apart from that faith, the Church is nothing at all. Dogmas, creeds, and doctrines, as well as structures, hierarchies and authorities, are merely the ways and means whereby the faithful can articulate and organize their belief. They do not define or constitute the Church itself. They simply express how that faith has been integrated into the various moments of history.

The Church, then, is a process. More specifically, it is the process whereby individuals come to believe in Jesus and add the weight of their belief to the furtherance of the process that is the Church. In this view the Church is not a stable, immutable institution that has existed since the time of Jesus, founded by him and protected by him from the changes of the world. The Church is the consequence of its first members' faith in Jesus and the subsequent faith that it inspired. In its dialogue with the world that faith takes new shapes, thus giving new shapes to the Church. In this sense, then, the Church is constantly changing and readapting according to the exigencies of the world. Because the world changes, the Church must change, too. Change is therefore not something merely to be tolerated, but something to be encouraged as important to the vitality and continuity of the Church. Fidelity does not consist in mere repetition. The Church can be faithful to the spirit of Jesus only within the process of each succeeding moment of history.

The Church as a process is also the Church as an organism in society. It is the consequence of the followers of Jesus related to each other by their faith in him. As the Church moves through history and increases its membership, the number of these faith-relations increases. The reality of the Church is always found in the faith-relation of its believers, in continuity with the faith-relation of believers at every moment in the Church's history. This is what Vatican II implies when it speaks of the Church as the people of God. Apart from its people, the Church is nothing at all.

Since the relationship of faith about which we are speaking is essentially a belief in Jesus, the entire structure of the Church is obviously larger than simply those who are card-carrying (or basket-contributing) members of a particular Christian sect. Furthermore, insofar as the meaning of that faith can be expressed in non-Christian ways by people of other backgrounds and cultures, they too can be included in a still larger concept of the people of God. The Church in its widest sense, then, is the entire community of men as related by the faith in God to which Christianity aspires in the name of the Lord Jesus. These levels of identification describe the Church as an organism.

A new model of the Church as processive and organismic would be difficult to define with dictionary precision. Its history is the manifestation of the spirit of Jesus in all of its variety and unpredictability throughout the Christian epoch. It is not the succession of the papacy or the formulation of creeds and dogmas. And its present moment is not lived only in church buildings. The Church is wherever two or more are gathered in faith to reiterate and reinterpret the importance of Jesus according to the inspiration of his spirit.

In Whiteheadian philosophy, the processive and relational aspects of reality are described in terms of nexūs of actual occasions. We have already defined a nexus as a set of actual occasions related to each other in time and space. The Church, then, is a nexus of its individual members in time and space. As a nexus, these individual elements are joined together in a single fabric, called the Church, or assembly of the people of God.

A nexus in which the component actual occasions are ordered among themselves in a certain way is called a "society." A nexus is a society when a certain identifying characteristic is a contributory component of each of the elements in that society. It is not sufficient that a class name can be applied to each element of the society. It is necessary that each element also incorporate within itself the same identifying characteristic as the other elements within that nexus. That is, each actual occasion of the nexus must prehend positively that characteristic which identifies the society as a whole.

The Church is a society as well as a nexus. Its claim to being a society rests upon the prehension of the importance of Jesus in each of its members. The Church is not merely the class name of all those who believe in the importance of Jesus. It is rather the consequence of that importance being prehended in each moment or occasion of its history. That is, the Church is a society in the technical Whiteheadian sense because its members prehend that importance from past members of the society and incorporate that importance into themselves. In this way the spirit of Jesus literally lives on in each of the members. Therefore, the Church, as a society, is a creative force in the environment, because its past is always the data for further becoming in faith. This further becoming occurs both in new members and in new understandings.

No society exists alone. Each is set in the context of a wider society which constitutes its environment. Without the wider context there could be no identifiable characteristic. The Church, therefore, is always in relation to what is not the Church. This interaction is the basis of its ecumenical interests and its pastoral mission. Both of these imply movement and change within the Church. The Whiteheadian model of inter-relatedness and process provides a convenient framework to explain the incorporation of new insights and the resultant growth within the Church, and the Church's influence on the world in general. In its ideal form, the evolution of the Church is an illustration of the evolution of reality: the many become one and are increased by one.

The identity of the Church according to the model we have been suggesting is not found in an essential definition of its nature as an institution, but in the function of its evolution. The Church is primarily a process, not a structure. That process has an identifying characteristic, but that characteristic is not a definition of the Church. This may seem like a small point to stress so frequently, but its implications for ecclesiology are vast. It spells the difference between looking at the Church as a substantial, structural reality which contains members who believe, and viewing the Church as an event moving through history, constantly evolving in its very make-up according to the shape that the belief of its members takes at a given moment in history and according to the way in which that belief finds expression in relation to the larger environment or culture where it is found.

The identifying characteristic is a way of conceptualizing what is important in the society, but it does not define the reality of the society. Its function lies not in the fact that it is conceptualized for purposes of an abstract definition, but in the fact that it is successively incorporated in an immanent way into the actual occasions that constitute the society. In other words, being a Christian makes a difference because belief in the importance of Jesus enters into the very composition of the actual occasions that constitute the life of a Christian. The Church is the consequence of their being Christians. One does not become a Christian by joining a Church.

The incorporation of the identifying characteristic in the elements of the society has two functions. It is the basis both for its survival as a society and for the intensity that it achieves. The art of survival, Whitehead suggests, is to be a rock.[2] It exists in its environment simply, continually reiterating the past to the present. Bare survival contributes a passivity and a sameness to a society. In contrast, intensity requires complexity, not simplicity. Elements are continually molded and kneaded into new shapes and forms. There is an active and creative appropriation of the past and of the immediate environment for the purpose of building the future. Intensity is the zest and flavor of life, and this is also an important ingredient for a society. Both survival and intensity are necessary in an organism, whether it be an actual occasion, a society of occasions, or the entire cosmos. Survival and intensity, reiteration and novelty—these are the dual elements in Jesus' own statement that upon a *rock* he would *build* the Church.

One might argue that a belief merely in the importance of Jesus is inadequate to be the identifying characteristic of the Church, and that a statement about the divinity of Jesus would be a better expression of what that importance means in the Christian tradition. The problem is precisely that such a statement is an expression, not a prehension. It states how Christians have traditionally expressed Jesus' importance, whereas the former deals with how they originally intuited the person of Jesus. Surely the divinity statement adds a new intensity to the faith. But as a statement it tends to generate other statements, which together take on a normative and exclusive character. A more simple description of the experience, without regard for how that experience has been expressed, promotes the survival dynamic by not limiting the possible expressions of that experience. Minimal statements expand the range of inclusion; maximal statements increase the depth. When the latter become the normative statements, exclusion inevitably results. The identifying characteristic of the Church with an eye to its survival mechanism should therefore be painted with a wide sweep of the brush, allowing the precisions of intensity to fill in the narrower, more aesthetically pleasing lines.

There is often a tendency for intensity to view survival with disdain. When intensity wins out at the expense of survival, rather than in harmony with it, definitions and statements of exclusion narrow the scope of the society. Such definitions and statements, issued in the interests of preserving internal purity, cause the society gradually to lose touch with the wider, "impure" environment in which it is located. Since no society can long remain independent of its surroundings, the demands of preserving purity can also effect societal suffocation.

The difficulty with the substance model of the Church is that intensity is generally won at the expense of survival. Dogmas, creeds and doctrines within the context of structure, hierarchy and authority express the intensity of the Church. These sometimes tend to cut the Church off from its environment, because they become the essential definition of the Church and the boundaries between inclusion and exclusion. A process-relational model of the Church also recognizes these elements as necessary for the Church's intensity factor, but the intensity factor serves as a characteristic, not as a definition of the Church. The definition of the Church, if indeed it can be defined at all, is always the people of the Church in the act of creating the Church. What they are creating is shaped by a common characteristic—their prehension of the importance of Jesus. Survival is not threatened by the variety of ways in which expressions of that faith introduce novelty into the process. In this way, survival is enhanced by intensity and novelty.

The process-relational model of the Church does not tend to isolate the Church from what is going on around it. It is ecumenical in the widest sense of the term. Just as no society exists in isolation from its envi-

ronment, so also the Church always finds itself tempo-
rally and spatially in the wider context of the world
and essentially inter-related with it. Because of this relatedness, the Church contributes itself to the world and
the world contributes itself to the Church.

The mode of contribution is always via the elements that constitute it. The Church as a society does
not contribute apart from the elements that constitute
it, although the weight of the elements working together may outweigh the collection of individual contributions. Rather, the Church contributes to the world
because, and merely because, its members contribute to
it. This is because the Church is a society of the faith of
the people of God. Apart from its people, there can be
no faith and no society.

The above describes *how* the Church contributes to
the wider environment. *What* it contributes is its in-
touch-ness with the importance of Jesus today. Therefore, the Church can never entertain a conflict between
relevancy and tradition. This is always a false dilemma.
The Church's relevance *is* its tradition. Just as an irrelevant Church is ultimately unfaithful to the spirit of its
foundation in Jesus, so also a Church disinterested in
its tradition is ultimately undermining the basis of its
faith. But the Church tradition is not a static, stable
past fact, repeated from epoch to epoch. It is past data
still shaping and forming the present by virtue of its
real inclusion in it.

IX

SACRAMENTS

While medieval theologians were wont to stress that man is a rational animal, contemporary theologians would probably prefer to say that man is a psychological animal. During this century we have become increasingly aware of the psychological dimension of man, and how his rationality is influenced and perhaps even conditioned by the world that surrounds him. Because he is psychological as well as logical, man is often persuaded by reasons that are not purely rational. He needs arguments that appeal to the heart as well as to the head. Emotions and feelings must be included in his theology as well as reasons and distinctions.

Although the full complexity of this aspect of man is only now being explored systematically, the basic truth about man's psychological make-up has been a part of his religious intuition for centuries. There is much primitive psychology in religion, and Christianity's sacramental system is a good example. It is hard to imagine how faith in Jesus could have lasted through the centuries without something more tangible than the New Testament and the abstract formulae of creeds and councils. In intuiting man's psychological needs and providing its followers with something concrete in the administration of the sacraments, Christianity showed true genius. Despite alterations in form and number, its sacraments have endured as manifestations of the continuing faith of Christians in every age and place of Christendom.

Sacraments are ways of getting in touch with the Jesus-event. They recall concretely and symbolically the faith Jesus inspired in his followers, and they become themselves occasions of gathering the faithful for new, creative expressions of their belief. One might say that they serve to mediate the past to the present. By "celebrating" the Jesus-event for each succeeding age of Christians, they have enabled Christianity to maintain its effectiveness.

Sacraments have been described in different ways in Christian theology. Probably the most familiar description is that of St. Thomas, who borrows St. Augustine's idea that sacraments are outward signs instituted by Christ causing inward grace. In Thomistic theology sacraments are primarily signs, but they are not ordinary signs, because they also cause what they signify. What they cause is grace, and this takes place both because the sacrament is properly performed (*ex opere operato*) and because the recipient is of good disposition (*ex opere operantis*).[1] A sacrament is properly performed when one uses the correct matter (material symbols) and the correct form (formal symbols, i.e., language). The recipient is of good disposition when he approaches the sacrament in the spirit of faith, intending to benefit from its graces.

Implied in the Thomistic approach is that a distinct divine intervention takes place every time the sacramental rite is performed. Given the divine institution of the sacraments by Jesus and given the necessity of an individual divine intervention, exact adherence to the prescribed formula of administration became the guarantee that a sacrament was efficacious. This led to an excessive preoccupation with rubrical precision. The validity of a sacrament was judged only according to its fidelity to the prescribed rubrics and in no way according to the intensity it inspired in its recipients. The result was a certain quasi-magic. As long as the prescriptions were fulfilled, grace automatically resulted, and the faithful were automatically enriched. The "filling-station" approach to sacraments became the common attitude: one came to the sacraments periodically to "fill up" again on grace.

It would be unfair to Thomism to claim that it is responsible for the unsophisticated application of its theology described above. Nevertheless, a return to the Thomistic system is probably not the best solution because its language, its concepts, and even its presuppositions sound very strange to contemporary ears. An explanation of sacraments more in tune with the psychological dimension of man would better suit our present mentality, and this is certainly not one of the strengths of Thomistic theology.

In contrast, process theology provides an interesting alternative, because it can speak in terms of sign and cause while also being sensitive to the importance of human feelings and the psychological dimension of man. In the process perspective, each sacramental action is both created by the community and creative of the community. As created by the community it presumes the prior faith of Christians and their desire to renew that faith. This is the function of the sacrament *ex opere operantis*: without the prior disposition of the believing community there can be no sacramental effect. As creative of the community, the sacrament leaves its influence on the faith of the believers and the process of the Church, whether it is performed well or poorly. This is its function *ex opere operato;* by the very performance of the sacrament the Church comes to grace (or dis-grace).

Sacraments can be described in Whiteheadian language as positive prehensions of the Jesus-event. Prehensions, as we have seen, are concrete "feelings" or "experiencings" of the past. Via prehensions the past contributes itself positively to the present and is immanently incorporated in what the present is becoming. As prehensions, then, sacraments not only remember Jesus and the faith of his followers. They also represent them concretely to the present. Technically, this is called "causal efficacy" in Whitehead's philosophy. Applied to sacraments, it means that the Jesus-event is causally efficacious during those occasions when the sacraments are administered in his name.

By the same token, the occasions of sacramental encounter are efficacious in the lives of its participants. We have already noted how sacraments are occasions of gathering the faithful, as well as occasions of re-presenting the Jesus-event. To the degree that the sacraments are performed well, i.e., they appealingly represent the Jesus-event to the faithful, they leave their positive impact upon those who have gathered. This is the sacrament's causal efficacy upon the Church and the way in which the presence of Jesus is dynamically continued. Taken together, this twofold causal efficacy demonstrates how process theology, like Thomistic theology, can affirm that sacraments cause what they signify.

Sacraments are signs as well as causes. They are signs because they are a common ground between the past and the present and because they provide a correlation between them. When we perceive something, we perceive it both as the result of its historical continuity and in its present immediacy. If the latter is in fitting correlation with the historical continuity, we readily interpret a meaning to it. Sacraments are signs because they bring together certain important moments of history and a certain contemporaneous event, and present a definite correlation between them. That is, they suggest the continuity between the Jesus-event and the occasions of sacramental action. In a sacrament, therefore, we perceive both an action and a reference, and we interpret a meaning from them.

The sacramental action need not be a literal replay of particular episodes in the life of Jesus. Indeed, such a literal repetition would be unfaithful to the present moment. An exact translation of an event from one culture to another always betrays the true nature of the event. *La traduction, c'est la trahaison!* Nevertheless, there must be enough common ground, in the form of common eternal objects and perceivable continuity, so that the correlation can be readily grasped.

The construction of sacramental ritual, therefore, is achieved through a delicate balance between reiteration and creativity. If the sign is to be efficacious in representing the historical Jesus-event, it must reiterate. If it is to be efficacious of itself in intensifying the event it signifies in the lives of those gathered about, it must also be creative. Good liturgy thus depends upon both fidelity to tradition and sensitivity to the needs of those gathered to participate.

Fidelity to tradition is the concern of the entire Church. Since sacraments are the way in which the presence of Jesus is maintained in the Church as a whole, the Church's future is dependent upon the way they are performed. If the Church is a process and sacraments are creative of that process, then the people of God have a vital concern in preserving their identifying characteristic through the administration of the sacraments. This is why a certain sameness is essential in liturgy, at least to the extent that liturgy celebrates in some way the importance of Jesus in the contemporary context. The survival dynamic of the Church depends upon this minimal fidelity to its tradition.

At the same time sensitivity to the needs of the faithful demands that liturgical celebrations be creative and meaningful. The events to be re-presented must have a purpose beyond the performance of the sacrament itself. The increasing use of themes in Masses and the construction of liturgies for particular community events are recent attempts to elicit more of the intensity dynamic in the Church. Ideally, such themes and liturgies should arise out of the needs and concerns of those gathered to perform the sacraments, since intensity can have its effect only to the extent that it touches them. This, of course, means that well-performed liturgy is well-prepared liturgy. Finding both the right medium and the right message for a particular group is a time-consuming undertaking. Abandonment of the "filling-station" spirituality, however, makes such efforts imperative.

In the practice of most Christian churches, and especially in Roman Catholicism, there has been a certain reluctance to admit emotion into liturgical celebrations. Expressions of feeling seemed out of place in man's dealings with God, because they were part of his lower nature and thus inferior to his intellect and will. The sterile liturgies that often resulted from this attitude seem to support the opinion of most modern psychologists that man cannot be so arbitrarily divided. The man who celebrates liturgy must celebrate it with his whole self, or he restricts the efficacy of the liturgy in his own life.

Process theology has an important corrective to suggest here. The way in which man gets in touch with the past is through his prehensions of the past. Now prehensions are fundamentally "feelings" or "experiencings" that re-create the past in one's present moment of existence. Feelings of this fundamental kind are, therefore, a necessary condition for fidelity to one's tradition. To abstract from the prehension or feeling of the past only its intellectual component is to strip the tradition of its very reality. We have a feel for tradition because feelings do come to us from tradition. Sacraments, which put us in touch with tradition, are the means whereby we recapture its fullness and allow it to fill us with new life.

Sacraments are privileged moments in the Church because they establish a privileged relation to Jesus. They are important moments to the believer because they collapse the time between him and the origins of his faith in order that that faith can be re-created in the new occasion in which the sacrament is performed. That is why it is imperative that sacraments be adequate signs and full expressions of what they represent.

The sense of the term "sacrament" as we have been using it here obviously can extend beyond the range of the seven official sacraments of Roman Catholicism. Any occasion that gathers two or more together to re-present and re-create the Jesus event and to renew the faith of those gathered is, in the wide sense, sacramental. A sermon, some moments of common prayer, or even a simple conversation that inspires can be sacramental in this sense. Liturgical worship is, of course, especially designed to be sacramental. The primordial sacrament for us is the Eucharist, because it is the most frequently used and most effective means of re-presenting the Jesus-event in a meaningful way. In the last few paragraphs of this chapter we shall attempt to explain the Eucharist, and the sacrament of baptism by which it is preceded, according to the spirit of process theology.

Thomistic philosophy defined the Eucharist in terms of the substances of bread and wine. At the moment when the words of consecration were correctly completed, the substances of bread and wine were "transubstantiated" into the body and blood of Jesus. The problem with this explanation in our age is that it is difficult to reconcile with our scientific sophistication. Upon scientific analysis, the so-called substance of bread is merely a mixture of carbohydrates, proteins and other elements, none of which can be properly called bread. Wine is just as much of a problem to identify substantially. If there is no substance of bread or wine, how can that substance change into the body and blood of Jesus?

Some contemporary theologians, using insights of existential philosophy and phenomenology, have suggested that the underlying reality of bread and wine is not substance, but meaning. Bread is bread because man has agreed to call a certain combination of baked elements "bread." When the words of consecration are repeated, this combination of baked elements is removed from the level of ordinary bread and assigned a new meaning in faith, according to the promise made by Jesus at the institution of the sacrament. This explanation of the Eucharist has been called "transignification" or "transfinalization."

In process philosophy there is no underlying reality of bread and wine that can be transubstantiated or transfinalized. The only realities are actual occasions, which are temporal as well as spatial. The best description of the Eucharist, then, is in terms of an event. What is transformed is not the substance or meaning of bread and wine, but the action that is performed. Jesus is made present again, or re-presented, by a sacramental event that corresponds to the Jesus-event. Except for the sacramental action there can be no Eucharist. Corresponding to the common expressions of the early Christians, the Eucharist is the "breaking of the bread" and the "sharing of the cup," not simply the bread and wine by themselves. It is the re-presentation of the Last Supper event in the new event of the Mass. The community, in causing the actions of the Mass to become sacramental, is itself transformed by that sacramental action to live at a new intensity and to continue the process of the Church.

Baptism is the event whereby a new member is incorporated into the community of faith. That is why the new liturgy of baptism in the Roman Catholic rite insists upon the presence of a representative group of the community. The person is becoming a member of the community, and a new relation is being established. The sacramental effect of the baptism event is therefore important both to the person and to the community. The community assures the person of its support in faith, and the person pledges his support in faith to the other members of the community. Jesus' own action of incorporating new members into the first Christian community is thus re-presented in the rite of baptism. The sign of the sacrament causes what it signifies. Through it the process of the Church continues to create and be created.

A description of the other sacraments would follow the same pattern, to a greater or lesser degree. A number of other liturgical or para-liturgical actions could also be explained in a similar manner. The number of sacraments has not been constant in the history of the Church, and there is no reason to believe that even the seven so defined as sacraments are to be considered as equally important. A clue in this regard comes from our Protestant brothers in Jesus. For most Protestants, baptism and the Eucharist have been retained, even while the other sacraments have been abandoned or restructured. The fact that in many segments of Roman Catholicism this same phenomenon is occurring suggests that perhaps there is something more fundamental and important in these two sacramental events than in the others. But on this subject process theology has nothing unique to contribute. It is content to observe the new developments in order to understand better the shape that the process we call the Church is taking in our time.

X

MORALITY

The new morality has been around for quite a while now, but it still manages to generate plenty of heated discussion, especially when the participants are parents and their adolescent children. No changes in our society have caused more fear and anxiety to the older generation than the numerous challenges to traditional moral standards. Contrary to what they had formerly been taught, moral standards do seem to change, and in fact have changed radically in one generation. Or, in the interests of precision, we might say that what has changed is the understanding of morality. While it is evidently not true to say that young people are less moral than their parents, it is quite true to say that what they understand morality to include or exclude is often very different.

The so-called new morality is quite simple in the minds of most young people. They hold two fundamental principles: (1) nothing can be decided unless you are in a concrete situation, and (2) it's O.K. as long as it doesn't hurt anybody. By this standard Vietnam was wrong because it was a concrete situation where people were being hurt and killed, and no abstract strategies of American foreign policy could justify it. Likewise, extra-marital sex cannot be condemned in itself; when both parties agree, there is no wrong because it is a pleasure that does not hurt anybody. In such a perspective the just-war theory of Augustine and the sexual restrictions of the Roman Catholic Church are equally unpersuasive, and, indeed, are themselves immoral!

In contrast, we generally hear the older generation arguing in the traditional way. Morality comes ultimately from God, according to his eternal law. When that law is revealed to us, or when it has been deduced by reason, we are constrained to obey its prescriptions. To live morally, one is not so much concerned with the situation as with the law. The situation is important only insofar as it enables one to know which law is applicable. The task of teaching us the law and helping us to apply it is the function of the state and the Church, and one can expect his reward or punishment in this life or in eternity, according to his obedience to civil and divine law respectively.

While these two descriptions may be oversimplified, they are detailed enough to illustrate the major strengths and weaknesses of each approach to morality. The new morality is more flexible and less confining. It permits one to reach reasonable decisions even where the law indicates otherwise. Responsibility rests upon the person who makes the decision; he cannot blame the law or the authorities for making him do what he did.

There are also weaknesses in the new morality. If no decision is valid outside of the concrete situation, what is it about the concreteness of the situation that suddenly enables one to choose wisely? It is precisely in moments of crisis where a decision is demanded that one often is unable to mobilize his powers of reflection to make a prudent choice. What his personal values are prior to the crisis and what previous reflection he can draw upon are always important determinative components in any decision. But if we admit the importance of pre-determined personal values in making a critical decision, does not this imply that one has some aim or purpose that gives meaning to those values and that directs his moral behavior? For what makes something a value is that it is seen to have more worth than something else, which is judged to have a lesser value, according to the overall aim or purpose one has chosen to pursue. So "leaving it up to the concrete situation" really doesn't suffice. Some guidelines are necessary for dealing with the situation, and these guidelines are precisely the abstract values, ideals, aims and purposes that are not, and can never be situational. Some kind of ethical standard will be at work in deciding how to handle a particular situation. To refuse to reflect seriously about that ethical standard until one finds himself in the concrete situation does not lead to purity of decision; it merely means that impulse will have a greater share than reason in the final outcome.

The other problem with the new morality is the principle that one must not hurt anybody. It sounds innocent enough, but as ethical principle it is too minimal to be of much use. For one thing, it is stated negatively and doesn't suggest any positive aims or directions one ought to strive for. Secondly, "anybody" presumably means "any human being." But an ethic that is limited to human beings is going to be somewhat inadequate in this age of ecological crisis. There has to be a way of judging the hurt we inflict on other *things*. This is a difficult problem, because we must continue to eat, to build homes, and to warm our bodies. Since every action ultimately affects and often hurts something, we cannot extend this principle to say, "as long as it doesn't hurt any*thing*." Some more sophisticated way of determining what kinds of hurts are tolerable, and what kinds are not tolerable must be found. Some of the hurts will be to man, at least in the form of fewer conveniences or luxuries. But we have passed the age where humanism can be the sole ethical criterion. We are too intertwined with nature as a whole, and too dependent upon it. New ethical theories must be sensitive to that fact.

On the other hand, the old morality is just as defective, and perhaps even more so. Its weaknesses have been so frequently subjected to the scrutiny of the new moralists that it will not be necessary to repeat them here, except in summary form. The new moralists argue that the old morality is too rigid and inflexible. It tends to enslave man to the law, rather than liberate him to act creatively in society. In the name of stability it often causes stagnation and immobility. Because it is centered on law, it has become the refuge of traditionalists seeking to preserve the status quo. Observance of the law is the final justification for conformity. As Whitehead once put it, "The defense of morals is the battle-cry which best rallies stupidity against change."[1]

However, the old morality cannot be discarded out of hand. Any system that has served for so many centuries must have something to say for itself. What it teaches is that we cannot get along without some ethical guidelines. Perhaps, in a quickly changing world where law always loiters behind the moral conscience of people, it is no longer right to judge the morality of actions exclusively according to the prescriptions of the law. But if the moral laws of the past can be understood in a new way, not as prescriptions to be followed but as values that the wisdom of history provides, then perhaps the old moralists can still teach the new moralists some important things.

The point of convergence between traditional morality and situational morality is in their attempts to articulate a set of values that can offer guidance in the task of building the future. Laws, when interpreted as principles or guidelines, can warn us about what we ought to avoid. The concrete situation can focus upon the immediate facts. But something more is needed. Our projections of the future demand some assessment regarding what kinds of things—given the new possibilities for science and technology—we really want to promote for the ages ahead. A philosophy of values, enriched by a dialogue among diverse ethical theorists, is thus indispensable for any ethics in the twentieth century. Process thought, because it is both metaphysical and flexible, can make an important contribution to this discussion.

"Value," says Whitehead, "is the outcome of limitation."[2] Limitation is the result of the selection by which an actual occasion is ultimately shaped. Only as a result of how it prehends its relevant past and gives it new focus does a new concrete occasion come into existence. Value is the intrinsic reality of the occasion, insofar as its own synthesis is unique and will have an impact upon further process.

Value, therefore, is always concrete and never realized except in individual actual occasions. It is the consequence of the particularity that emerges and then contributes itself as new data to the world. We can, of course, abstract from concrete values to speak of value systems and value hierarchies. These are simply ways in

which the human mind operates to understand and coordinate what is happening in reality and to decide what
is truly important.

Morality is "the control of process so as to maximize importance."[3] "Importance" is another technical
word in the Whiteheadian vocabulary. Briefly, it occurs
when the intensity of feeling leads to publicity of expression.[4] In the context of morality, it means that
there must be a constant transcending of the present
moment toward public novelty and interest. It is the
greatness of experience that goes beyond itself. Occasions that contribute greatness of experience to the
on-going process of the universe achieve greatness of
value. That is, each occasion should aim at new and interesting possibilities, unique harmonies and contrasts.
An occasion's contribution to the future consists in how
it makes new data available. The future is the final
judge of whether it achieved success. In the words of
Whitehead, "The effect of the present on the future is
the business of morals."[5]

There is no question that the major impetus of
Whitehead's ideas on morality are future-oriented. A
less obvious but equally important dimension to his
ethical thinking arises from the inter-relational character of reality. Morality is inseparably linked with our
position in the whole. It is never a private affair, done in
isolation from the rest of reality. Every moral decision
has some impact on the whole and bears the weight of
that responsibility. Therefore, the general good and the
individual good can never be in conflict, because both
share a common world and a common future. Individual
interests must always be harmonized with the more general interests. This is a significant implication to his
statement that morality consists in maximizing impor-

tance. Importance is always determined by the individual occasion's impact upon the future taken as a whole. For in the literal sense, an occasion has no future except insofar as it is integrated into wider perspectives and newer horizons.

Where process thought goes beyond the humanistic ethics that have been so popular in our time is in its concern not only for the unity of mankind, but for the integration of all reality. There is an essential inter-relatedness about all of nature that transcends the needs of the human species, and there can be no separation of the latter from the former at any step of ethical deliberation. The concern of morality is reality, not merely man. For man is not his own end. He dies, and his civilizations die. Were man the ultimate purpose of the universe, creation would have to be judged woefully inefficient. Clearly, something more is at stake, even in this age of environmental pollution, than the survival of man. In the final analysis, the survival of the universe is a value of greater importance, because from it the processes at work in reality can continue to create a history.

In light of this ethical perspective, what can we abstract from the concrete values we are given in each emerging occasion of reality? Can we suggest some abstract values and aims that are truly worthy of human efforts?

Whitehead suggests that the aims of a civilized society are a "fineness of feeling" and a "generality of understanding."[6] We might note that these aims are intrinsic to the process and do not define values apart from the process itself. Both are expressions of what process, as process, is about. The first aim of morality, then, is the continuance of process in its maximal effect. This occurs at the level both of individuality and of society. Each individual occasion contributes its fineness of feeling, and the whole achieves a generality of understanding. For process thought, the individual and the totality are equally of value. Therefore, morality is compromised when there is the totalitarianism of the whole over the parts or when there is the anarchy of the parts with respect to the whole. Morality never chooses between the welfare of the particular or of the communal. It must always strive toward their integration in a way that values both the uniqueness of individuality and the harmony of generality.

While the first business of morals is to safeguard experience and to continue the process, Whitehead does make some suggestions about the qualities that ought to be furthered by process, and here we see especially the Platonic character of his thought. In his book *Adventures of Ideas* he lists five eternal objects: truth, beauty, adventure, art and peace. Curiously, good and right are not included in his list. The main reason is simply that these terms are so overworked that their meanings have become quite imprecise. Instead he chooses these five as qualities which do have meaning, and which are sufficiently clear and comprehensive so as to include in a general way what man actually finds valuable in process.

Whitehead defines truth much like Thomas Aquinas. It is the conformation of appearance to reality.[7] A truth relation is constituted when the content of two connected facts participate in the same general pattern. There can be many kinds of truth relations, thus justifying the use of the term both for art and mathematics, as well as for concrete impressions and abstract speculations. Sense perception is the primary way of attaining truth, because from it appearances are usually derived clearly and distinctly, despite occasional failures or interferences. Thus the things we perceive provide steady values, and these are incorporated into the subjective form of the prehending occasion and become part of the data out of which new occasions emerge.

Beauty goes beyond truth in the spontaneous adaptations of some of the factors prehended by an occasion of experience. The adaptations arise in pursuit of a certain aim, in which intensity of feeling and conformity to a common pattern combine for the attainment of harmony. That is, there is the perfection of the subjective form arising out of the variety of prehensions in such a way that the component feelings do not inhibit each other from achieving their ideal inter-relation. Beauty is thus wider and more fundamental than truth, because it deals not only with the conformation of appearance to reality, but also with the perfection of the subjective forms that are shaped by their interrelation.

Art is the purposeful adaptation of appearance to reality. The achievement of art thus depends upon the perfection of man, as he has been shaped by beauty. But perfection is not a static concept. Like civilization itself, it must always promote novelty and originality. When these cease to be important, civilization dies. Thus, Whitehead includes adventure as a necessary quality, lest inspiration yield to mere repetition. Finally, peace, the harmony of harmonies, is a call to go beyond limitations and beyond the self, without denying the self. Peace thus seeks to achieve the integration of order and love. It is the positive quality that crowns the "life and motion" of the soul.[8]

The final question we must ask is whether there is in the universe any general drive toward the realization and perfection of these five qualities. Is there a greater and more perfect conformity of appearance and reality revealed in the movement of history? In other words, is a constant progress inherent in the nature of process? For process thinkers of a Whiteheadian bent, the answer to these questions is less optimistic than it is for the disciples of Pierre Teilhard de Chardin. Process is a metaphysical principle of reality, but there is no corresponding principle of progress. Thus, there is no guarantee of improvement in history.

Whiteheadians generally eschew the claim of inherent progress. First, it would be difficult to establish absolute norms of progress, and norms that might seem sufficient for the best self-interests of man may not necessarily serve the best interests of reality as a whole. To absolutize human norms simply because they are human seems rather presumptuous in the wider perspective of things. Another reason is that our experience does not indicate that even on the human level process has resulted in progress. By human standards, scientific and technological advances can probably be called progress, and yet there do not seem to be any similar advances in moral living. Man is just as likely to occasion discord as harmony, selfishness as love.

What our experience tells us is that change is not necessarily improvement, and that in the moral order every new possibility for good is simultaneously a possibility for evil. The size of good and evil grow apace. Scientists and technologists have enabled us to understand the finitude of our world and our essential interdependence with the forces that constitute it. But they have not—and cannot—provide us with the resolve to integrate ourselves into it. This is the domain of morals. It is today a frightening domain because of our knowledge. In our individual occasions of experience we are collectively deciding the very fate of process on this planet, and the size of this moral predicament is truly overwhelming. It is perhaps so overwhelming that it is beyond the scope of any one of us to comprehend.

That is why the new morality and the old morality, taken individually or together, are inadequate. More is at stake than can be answered by a situational analysis and an appeal to past wisdom. What is also needed is a vision of the future as an integrated totality and a sensitivity for the values that will get us there. This will not come from a commitment to seek out the evil and overcome it. Perhaps now more than ever, the Don Quixotes are irrelevant because of the magnitude of evil and the increasing number of evil possibilities. Nor will it come from an attempt to isolate evil and reject it, situation by situation, as one threads his way through the choices of life. No corporate good of any size can be achieved by such piecemeal, individualized efforts. Instead we must ask the question: How can we collectively look evil in the eye, accept its reality, and undertake to incorporate it into a larger good? Process is made up of everything in the past, however it is judged morally. If quality and size are to be squeezed from the relentless cadence of process, we must harness evil into our service. This is possible only when the good toward which we strive is truly large enough, important enough, and holy enough to lure us enthusiastically into the enterprise.

XI

IMMORTALITY

The ultimate mystery of life is death. Science and philosophy can tell us a lot about life, but when the final moment of life has passed us by, they must abandon us to our faith. Death transcends the powers of reason and shrouds itself in ineffability. Despite this eternal verity, there is presently a surge of interest in death and in the speculation about what, if anything, occurs after death. Inter-disciplinary courses are being taught in colleges and numerous new books and articles are being published dealing with the topic. What makes this enterprise so fascinating is that there are no criteria for determining which opinions are right and which are wrong. Spiritualists and rationalists both contribute their evidence and compare notes, but in the final analysis the mystery always remains.

Traditionally the Church has answered this question for its faithful with its teaching on the four last things: death, judgment, heaven and hell. At the moment of death, each soul is called to a particular judgment by God. As a consequence of the way one lived on earth, the soul is then determined for a heaven of eternal happiness with God or a hell of everlasting fire. Since the presence of God is reserved only for the worthy, imperfections and lesser evils in one's life have to be "worked off" before the beatific vision is possible. This intermediate state of purification is a place of temporary suffering, called purgatory. Finally, for those souls never officially admitted to membership and grace in the Church, a fourth place, called limbo, allows them the fullness of natural happiness, but without the vision of God.

There is, of course, no way to dispute the Church's teaching, nor is there any way apart from faith that it can be proved. For many theologians today, however, the doctrine is too intertwined with ancient culture, tradition and myth to be literally credible. Their recent reflections on the subject have resulted in drawing together ideas from anthropology, psychology and philosophy, as well as theology, in order to profit from new insights regarding the counsel that reason can offer to faith in clarifying the issue for the individual believer.

In the absence of indisputable evidence, the theologian too must ultimately make up his mind about an issue according to what he believes. If he is honest with himself—and hopefully most theologians are—his belief will be formed from the best evidence he can muster. But in the matter of death and immortality, none of his evidence can be verified. It is not surprising, therefore, that theologians, even within a single school of thought such as process theology, will argue a variety of positions regarding death and immortality. In fact, among process theologians such a diversity does indeed exist.

Whitehead himself was somewhat ambiguous on the subject. He does deal with death in a way that is logical and coherent in his theoretical synthesis and in a way that is open to a variety of imagery for pastoral purposes. The question of the afterlife, however, is left unresolved. For Whitehead, dying (or to use his term "perishing") is the antithesis of emerging, and each is continually occurring in every moment in every bit of reality. Only in the constant ebb and flow of emerging and perishing is change and enrichment possible. Perishing, therefore, is just as essential to the world as emerging.

In his essay on "Immortality"[1] Whitehead says that there are two abstract worlds, the "World of Value" and the "World of Activity." Neither is explainable except in terms of the other. Value can only be explained in terms of its realization in concrete actual occasions as they emerge and perish. Thus, "value" is always experienced as "values." Values are concrete, individual and unique contributions to future actualities. The realization of a particular moment of actuality is likewise the realization of a particular value, and this becomes part of the data for the succeeding moments of actuality. Values derived from the past are thus immanently incorporated into each emerging occasion. This is what Whitehead means by "immortality." Nothing that is of value is ultimately lost. Apart from such immanent incorporation, nothing could be preserved, and "value" itself would have no ultimate meaning.

This understanding of value is exactly parallel to Whitehead's notion of God. God, like every actual entity, is di-polar, reflecting both the mental and the physical, both the World of Value and the World of Activity. These two aspects in the divinity are, as we have seen, called God's primordial and consequent natures. Just as God, if he is to be actual, must be really related to the world and allow it to be incorporated into himself, so also the World of Value, if it is to be more than pure abstraction, must be realized in the World of Activity.

That is why value, in its concrete reality, is none other than the concrete elements of process. God embodies this in himself in his consequent nature, and offers it back to the world in each emerging occasion. To put it another way, the world adds activity to God and God adds value to the world.

The perishing of an actual occasion, therefore, need not be its extinction. Rather, it can be understood as a kind of switching of modes. Whereas in the emerging of an actual occasion God's immanence is felt in the incorporation of value, in its perishing that actual occasion is felt immanently in God as a fuller realization of the divinity. In this way the occasion continues to be felt in the formation of the future. Death, then, is emphatically not a passing into nothingness. Instead, it is immanent incorporation into God, in whom each actuality is experienced everlastingly for its own uniqueness and individuality. In dying, one "gets out of the way" of the present in order to be available to the future in a new way.

Does this doctrine of immortality, which Whitehead calls "objective immortality," correspond to the faith expectations of those who seek the reassurance of an afterlife, a place of eternal happiness, or a heaven? In some fundamental ways, at least, I think that it does. The basis for their belief is the impossibility of man's conceiving of himself as not being. The one absolute and certain experience that endures throughout his entire life is the experience of being in the present, recalling the past, and anticipating a future. One experiences a profound continuity with oneself in space and time.

Everyone has moments of unconsciousness where his experience of the world around him is temporarily interrupted. The most common example is sleep. But one always awakes to find himself the same person he was when he slumbered. There is an experience of the continuity of the self as far back as the memory permits. To think of this continuity as being abruptly and completely terminated is almost impossible to imagine or accept. This is the reason why man so often seeks to find a place and a time for himself after his death. That place can be a paradise free from the evils and insecurities of earthly existence, or it may simply be a place in the records of history or the lives of one's offspring. However he imagines it, it gives him some extension in time in which to maintain the continuity of self into the future.

This problem is acute in Western culture where one must reconcile death and immortality with lineal time. For lineal time, unlike cyclical time, implies an ending, termination or death, or at least a state of permanence, where time (and therefore change) is no more. Hence the common Western belief that once the final state of man has been reached, the world of activity is effectively excluded from his existence. This is just as true for those who believe that their personal extinction is permanent in death as it is for those who anticipate personal salvation in a heaven where suffering and sin are no more. In both cases, death is a permanent thing, and the forces of change are no longer relevant. The alternative to total annihilation for Western man is bare existence in an absolutely unchanging condition!

The belief of permanency after death has always been one of the difficulties of the Christian doctrine of heaven. On the one hand, Christian tradition holds that at the moment of death the eternal fate of the person is irretrievably sealed. Heaven is eternal happiness and hell is eternal punishment. In traditional thought this is necessary, because if the happiness is to be perfect, it cannot be threatened by change. Since the possibility of change is itself the cause of insecurity, perfect happiness is realizable only in the state of total security and stability. So, the Christian believes in the permanence of his final state.

But what possible meaning can be assigned to *experience* if it does not involve change? To experience is to take account of things outside the self and to allow them to affect the self, and this implies undergoing some change in the self. What we experience becomes a part of us. This necessarily alters the reality of the continuity that is the self, and it implies an absence of certitude about the future. Consequently, when personal experiences are admitted as part of the belief in heaven, the belief in the absolute changelessness of the afterlife is put into serious question. Thus, the dilemma. Either personal experience is retained, in which case the series of actual occasions constituting the self continues, and change is still possible, or personal experience is abandoned in favor of permanency, in which case immortality can only consist in a completed and non-experiencing self, whose existence consists in being experienced by another as an objectively immortal actuality.

The openness of Whitehead's thought on this point permits an explanation of the religious hereafter according to either possibility, and this is why process theologians often differ among themselves without abandoning their fidelity to the process system. We will begin with an explanation of the latter possibility, since this is a more direct application of Whitehead's own doctrine of "objective immortality." Here the emphasis is on permanency. What one was during life, especially during the final moments of life, determines what one is eternally. In this interpretation, the series of actual occasions that constitutes the continuity of the self throughout one's personal history culminates in one final occasion in which that history is synthesized. The entire continuity, but especially this final synthetic occasion in the continuity, is experienced by God and becomes a part of the data of God's own actuality. In this way each person is immortalized everlastingly in God, retaining permanently his own uniqueness and individuality, and contributing that uniqueness as data to a fuller appreciation of value and novelty for the future. However, this interpretation does not allow for any further subjective experiences or subjective change.

One can also argue for the possibility of "subjective immortality" using the thought of Whitehead.[2] In this interpretation the series of actual occasions that constitutes the continuity of the self is not interrupted or terminated by death; it only changes the environment in which it does its experiencing. The ordinary environment for the experiencing self is the body. However, there is no necessary reason why the series of actual occasions that constitutes the self cannot continue in some other non-material environment. Hence, death can be understood as the detachment of that dominant series of actual occasions we recognize as the self from the many supportive material series which constitute the human body. The new environment is the consequent nature of God, where the serial reality of the self continues to experience and to change, but without any direct attachment to the material world.

Given the Whiteheadian frame of reference, both of these interpretations are philosophically consistent within themselves, even though they may not be reconcilable with each other. Therefore, the decision which to choose in articulating one's belief depends upon the belief itself. This can actually be a significant advantage to the process theologian. Unlike other theological questions, which can be studied and discussed at leisure, the issue of immortality often arises in the context of a sudden personal tragedy. At such moments, the theologian would like to be able to provide an immediate, clear and definitive answer to comfort the dying or the bereaved. But in fact he must embarrassingly reply that there is no certain knowledge about what happens on the other side. There is only the assurance of one's personal faith.

Even the assurance of faith, however, must demonstrate a certain credibility. This means that it must seem reasonable to the one who believes. At this point the theologian can perhaps be of some practical help. Even while not being able to offer certitude, he can suggest reasons why the faith of the believer is plausible, whether that faith be in the literal continuance of subjective experiencing in a heaven or hell, or in some kind of objective permanence in human history. Thus, in those cases where the person does not want a reaffirmation of the traditional symbols about life after death in his particular circumstances, the appropriate theological explanation is Whitehead's "objective immortality." This option can be illustrated by religious statements suggesting that a goodness is never lost, that the world is permanently enriched by the past, and that God himself is magnified because of the goodness of each human person. On the other hand, process theology can also assist one who is committed to a more literal belief in the traditional teachings. Since his major concern is an anxiety about the future, he can be offered some assurances about his personal continuity within the framework of "subjective immortality." Here some possible religious statements may—with an underlying theological consistency—suggest that when a person dies he is taken up into God for an evaluation of his life, that he will be able to experience the effect that his life had on the world, and that he will have the opportunity to enjoy the good he helped to realize.

Is this a theological cop-out? Is it honest for a theologian simply to provide a set of reasons for whatever faith-option is proffered him? The answer to that question is both yes and no. Insofar as he attempts to be of service to human needs, the theologian may well decide that a moment of personal tragedy or crisis is not the moment to expose the differences between mystery and myth. In this capacity, the theologian is acting as minister, or as the scholarly aid to the minister. As such, he may in certain situations need to call upon theological reasons that are possibly not in accord with his own belief. The service function of the theologian, therefore, may include the formulating of a rationale for theological positions that he would not personally hold.

This need not compromise the theologian in his capacity as pure scholar. He can and should speak out honestly, in the ordinary course of his work, regarding the conclusions that he has come to in his quest for a theological understanding of the issue. The theologian, therefore, actually functions in two capacities: as a scholarly aid to the minister and as a ruthless seeker for truth. The advantage of process theology is that both functions can be adequately discharged in the matter of death and immortality from the single perspective of Whiteheadian thought.

The richness of process theology is such that it provides a solid philosophical framework for a great diversity of human experience and belief, and it is a helpful means of synthesizing them in interesting, creative new ways. It can account for, and indeed deepen, the thinking of traditionalist and liberal alike. Sometimes it can also be a useful instrument for translating between their different interpretations of their experiences of reality and their options of faith. These are the fundamental responsibilities of theology on behalf of faith: to understand, to support, and to deepen. For this task, process theology is very well suited.

XII

THEOLOGY
AND RELATIVITY

For many theologians any talk of relativity as adding something significant to their work is immediately rejected as a professional "no-no." Theology deals with what is most absolute in reality—God, man, and the eternal truths. If theology cannot offer man the absolutes of life, then no absolute standards of truth and morality are possible at all. Man is left hopelessly at sea, with neither rudder for direction nor a final port in which to drop anchor.

As one can see from the previous chapters, the process theologian does not share this anxiety about relativity. Indeed, many of the concepts with which he works are based upon the assumption of relativity. This does not mean that everything is arbitrary and man can believe and act on his whim or fancy. The notion of relativity that process theology employs is that all reality is inter-related in space and time, and that no single real entity has a prior absoluteness that stands outside the process of reality as a whole. Relativity thus contrasts with absoluteness in that it rejects the availability of any privileged moment or point of view from which everything can be finally and objectively evaluated. For the relativist, there is no way to set up criteria by which one moment or perspective can be more objectively valid than any other. The closest we can get to such objectivity is the judgment of reality as a whole upon any one of its parts.

What makes a moment or perspective privileged, then, is not any intrinsically determinable superiority, but the wide acceptance of its claim to privileged status. If or when that acceptance is eroded, the special status is diminished at the same time. According to this interpretation, then, the basis of Christianity is not found in the absolute uniqueness of Jesus as second person of the Trinity, but in the acts of faith that Jesus inspired and has continued to inspire in his own person throughout the centuries. The significance of Jesus can only be understood in relation to his followers.

The same is true of God. If he is serious about the reality of God, the process theologian will want to explain how God and the world are inter-related and how the significance of God is derived from the world. Process theologians, therefore, generally hold that God is in some sense dependent upon the world and that in that sense he is subject to the changes that take place in the world. Hence, God, like the world, is temporal.

These are the two most important instances where process theology causes difficulty for the Christian believer. It seems to do violence both to his affirmation of the divinity of Jesus and to his belief in the absolute immutability of God. The reason for this difficulty, however, is probably more a question of philosophy than a difference of faith. The traditional Christian belief regarding both the divinity of Jesus and the immutability of God is formulated in a set of static, non-temporal categories that give the impression of a certain absoluteness about these matters which is heedless of their relation to the temporal. Jesus, if he is God, has to be God eternally, and God, if he is truly God, has to be perfect eternally. The philosophical presuppositions implied in these statements have come to be accepted with the same act of faith that affirms the reality of God and the importance of Jesus.

The underlying philosophical position of traditional theology and its difference from the presuppositions of process thought can perhaps best be illustrated when we analyze the meaning of "perfect" and see its application to the Christian idea of God. For ages of Greek-educated Western minds, "perfect" referred only to a being in which there was no further possibility of improvement. The perfect being was one that could not be surpassed in any way with regard to its perfection. Change was therefore antithetical to perfection. It was the admission that imperfection existed either before the change or after it. Thus, a being that changed could not be called perfect, because it had not reached the optimum of its perfection, or because it did not have the guarantee of the permanence of its perfection.

The difficulty with the traditional interpretation is that improvement and growth are also perfections. That is, something that can grow or improve is more perfect than one that cannot. If, therefore, something is perfect in the traditional sense of being unchangeable, then it has lost the perfections of growth and improvement. There are, in other words, processive perfections as well as static ones. If God is truly perfect, he must exemplify both kinds of perfection. This means that a God who can grow and improve upon himself is more perfect than a God who remains static and unchanging, while other elements of reality are growing and improving.

The incorporation into God of both the static perfections and the processive perfections is the great achievement of Charles Hartshorne. In his writings he distinguished between absolute perfection and relative perfection. The former is applied to a being that is "unsurpassable in conception or possibility even by itself"; the latter obtains when the being is "unsurpassable except by itself."[1] It is the latter concept that is important for process theologians. It means that, in addition to imperfectible perfections, which are static, there are also perfectable perfections, which are dynamic. Given the temporal frame of reference, relative perfections do not and need not imply imperfection, which is the absence of a perfection that should be present at that time. It simply means that something which reaches a perfection relative to the rest of reality in one moment of time can be further perfected at a future moment of time.

When we apply this distinction to God, we can describe him as perfect if he has absolute perfection and/or relative perfection in all respects, and imperfection in no respect. This is another way of saying that God is perfect at every given moment of time. There is never anything imperfect in him at any moment, and at no time is he ever surpassable by any other being. However, he is capable of improving upon and surpassing himself. This is the way in which he relates himself concretely to the world: the realization of its values increases the values in him. It is also the way in which the world can relate itself to God: it can call him a "living God" because he can love, suffer and change. What happens in the world does make a difference to God, but without gainsaying his perfection in the process.

Traditional theology has always had a difficulty reconciling this belief in the personal nature of God with its belief in his absolute otherness, precisely because persons are relational realities and never absolutely other. This has created a series of questions that are literally unanswerable in the philosophical framework of that theology. For example, how is an absolute or "Supreme Being" really able to love in a personal way? If God loves each of us individually, must he not share our helplessness and powerlessness to deal with the forces of evil with which we must struggle in our lives? Yet, if he is perfect, how can he really be affected by the consequences of the imperfections and evils of the world?

The contribution of process theology to Christian faith is that in its perception the Christian does not have to compromise his belief that God is personal and loving for the sake of his belief in the perfection of God. Because of its philosophical presuppositions, it can explain divine love in terms that are fully compatible with our human experience of love, and it can explain divine perfection in terms that correspond to our own experience of change and growth.

The process theologian sees God's love as personal, extending to each actual entity individually and freely. God does not impose a particular destiny as a condition for proffering his love. Instead, by reason of his love, he offers the full range of possibilities without moral or religious imperatives, so that each entity can choose for itself what it will become. Freedom is essential to love, and when conditions are attached to the giving of love, they compromise the fullness of that love. God, as the perfect lover, does not attach any such conditions. Furthermore, genuine love not only wills the freedom of the beloved. It also accepts the consequences of that freedom. It must be willing to suffer and rejoice, initiate and acquiesce, give and receive. It must allow itself to be changed by that love. The God who truly loves, therefore, is a God who must also suffer and rejoice, initiate and acquiesce, give and receive. He must allow himself to be changed by that love.

Traditional theology sometimes speaks of God as suffering, rejoicing, or interacting in other ways with his creatures. The use of such terms is justified as anthropomorphisms—man's way of speaking about God in the absence of any language adequate to divine things. But while such language is tolerated, it is not applicable to God as he really is, because God cannot be affected by what happens in the world.

Process theology takes a different position. As the late Daniel Day Williams has written,[2] the very essence of love requires individuality, freedom, action, suffering and causality. The fact that biblical images attribute such love to God requires that Christians give them serious consideration as actual characteristics of God. Indeed, the biblical insight about God is precisely that he is more than an abstract, philosophical Being. He is the God of love, the God that Jesus called "Father." To maintain that the essential qualities of love are merely anthropomorphic ways of speaking about God questions whether God's love is truly love in any human understanding of the word.

If God is truly personal and living, his love for us must correspond to the way in which we understand love for each other. When a person takes on the personality of God, therefore, divine love is realized and incorporated into human affairs. This, as we have seen, is the explanation for the divinity of Jesus. Divine love had to grow and develop in him, much as it does in each of us. But unlike us, this love in Jesus continued to increase at every moment of his life, so that at every moment he was as perfect as he could be at that moment. He was like us in all things but sin.

In this context, it is not necessary to locate Jesus' divinity in an eternal pre-existence with God. This doctrine was important to the Greek-oriented theologians and Church Fathers who were unable to explain the perfection of Jesus in any other way than absolute perfection. Their decision to dogmatize this teaching reflected their concern for the uniqueness of Jesus, not for a philosophical statement about the nature of perfection. Since that time, however, many new insights have been added to human thought. If, for example, we accept relativity as an appropriate explanation of reality, then God is related to the world as a changing Becoming, and Jesus is related to God as a changing, growing person. The divinity of Jesus is thus located in the fact that his change and growth always realized concretely the most complete incorporation of divine love in his life. Thus, he was always perfect: as a human person he was unsurpassable in divine perfection in conception or possibility, except by himself. That is, he had relative perfection in every respect.

Do we do violence to Church doctrine and our traditions when we interpret God and Jesus in this way? Are we not taking rather bold liberties with the pronouncements of popes and councils down through the ages? For many, the answer will undoubtedly be in the affirmative. And for this reason, they will reject process theology and its explanations of the faith. For others, however, fidelity to the Church and to its traditions is not attained by faith in formulae, or even by the exigency of reconciling new ideas with old formulae. For these latter, fidelity consists in adherence to the fundamental experience of the early Church about Jesus and the God he proclaimed. Expressions are indeed important, but they are never more than expressions. The faith of the Church is found in the souls of Christians who from time to time try to articulate what they believe in various expressive forms. The Spirit speaks to man's soul, not to his verbiage. What man has written in the past as his Scriptures and as his dogmatic statements were expressions that more or less captured the experience of faith that was his at a particular moment in time. For this reason they are respected and reverenced, but they are not definitive expressions of the faith experience. The Spirit is always free to do what it will.

If our God is living, surely the Spirit is living also. It still speaks to the soul of man, but it speaks in new ways and with new words. This means that doctrine and tradition must be expected to grow, take on new forms, and find expression in new ideas. The discernment of spirits is not in the comparison of one set of words with another set of words, or even of one idea with another idea. The manifestation of the Spirit is to human experience, not to human expression. Discernment, therefore, is in the comparison of one faith experience with another faith experience, and in the concrete way in which that faith manifests itself in living. By their fruits you shall know them.

The process experience of Christian faith is certainly not alien to the experience expressed in the tradition. It is basically the experience of the inter-relatedness of reality through time. God, Jesus, the Church, and the other elements of Christian theology are understood and interpreted in that perspective. Love is central to the process perspective, much as it has been for all Christians since the time of John the Evangelist. Significantly, love is itself a relational concept. Love is not possible, or even conceivable, in isolation. It requires relatedness. To say that God is Love, as John does, implies that his fundamental character is that of relation to the world. If God is Love, he can exist only with a world and in a world. He is not possible, or even conceivable, in isolation from the world. And if indeed God actively manifests himself to the world through a man or through a Church, that manifestation will be characterized by love and thus by relatedness. This is what Jesus is, and this is what, hopefully, the Church continues to become.

But this is not yet the end of the story. Life goes on. The Church is still living, just as we are and God is. Process is still operative, and the world is still in labor as it struggles to bring forth the Christ in new ways. We are, in our century, very much aware of that process and very committed to new ways. It is the spirit of our age. Perhaps it is also the Spirit inspiring our age. It is in this spirit that process theology is born and offers its contribution to a continuing and deepening understanding of our Christian faith.

NOTES

Preface

   1. New York: Bobbs-Merrill, 1971.
   2. New York: Newman Press, 1971.

Chapter II

   1. The discussion in this chapter is based upon White-head's "Categorial Scheme," as outlined in *Process and Reality* (New York: The Macmillan Company, Free Press Paper-back edition, 1969), pp. 22-35.
   2. *Ibid.*, p. 26.

Chapter III

   1. For an excellent discussion of this issue, cf. Abraham H. Maslow,° *Religions, Values and Peak-Experiences* (New York: Viking Press, 1964).
   2. Alfred North Whitehead, *Religion in the Making* (New York: World Publishing Company, Meridian Books, 1960), p. 16.
   3. *Ibid.*, p. 115.
   4. Alfred North Whitehead, *Adventures of Ideas* (New York: The Macmillan Company, Free Press Paperback edition, 1967), p. 266.
   5. *Ibid.*, p. 285.
   6. *Religion in the Making, op. cit.*, p. 137.
   7. *Ibid.*, p. 59.
   8. *Process and Reality, op. cit.*, p. 19.
   9. Alfred North Whitehead, *Science and the Modern*

World (New York: The Macmillan Company, Free Press Paperback edition, 1967), p. 192.

Chapter IV

1. *Process and Reality, op. cit.,* p. 39.
2. *Ibid.,* p. 408.
3. *Ibid.,* p. 413.

Chapter V

1. Cf., for example, his two books, *A Christian Natural Theology* (Philadelphia: Westminster Press, 1965) and *God and the World* (Philadelphia: Westminster Press, 1969).
2. *Process and Reality, op. cit.,* p. 413.
3. *Ibid.,* p. 410.

Chapter VI

1. Alfred North Whitehead, *Modes of Thought* (New York: The Macmillan Company, Free Press Paperback edition, 1968), p. 161.
2. *Adventures of Ideas, op. cit.,* p. 208.
3. *Process and Reality, op. cit.,* p. 187 and p. 413.

Chapter VIII

1. For a fuller explanation of some of the ideas in this and the following chapter, see Bernard Lee's *The Becoming of the Church* (New York: Newman Press, 1974).
2. Alfred North Whitehead, *The Function of Reason* (Boston: Beacon Press, 1958), p.4.

Chapter IX

1. Although this distinction, to the best of my knowledge, does not appear as such in the writings of St. Thomas, it is suggested by a similar distinction in the *Summa Theologica*, III, 62, 1 and 4. Nevertheless, it has been popularized in this form

in the commonly used high school religion texts during the past generation. Thus it has become the accepted Thomistic teaching on the subject for most American Catholics.

Chapter X

1. *Adventures of Ideas, op. cit.*, p. 268.
2. *Science and the Modern World, op. cit.*, p. 94.
3. *Modes of Thought, op. cit.*, pp. 13-14.
4. *Ibid.*, p. 8.
5. *Adventures of Ideas, op. cit.*, p. 269.
6. *Ibid.*, p. 282.
7. *Ibid.*, p. 241.
8. *Ibid.*, p. 285.

Chapter XI

1. Published in *The Philosophy of Alfred North White-head*, Paul Arthur Schilipp, ed. (New York: Tudor Publishing Co., 1951), pp. 682-700.
2. Cf. David Griffin, "The Possibility of Subjective Immortality in Whitehead's Philosophy," *University of Dayton Review*, VIII, 3, pp. 43-56.

Chapter XII

1. Charles Hartshorne, *Man's Vision of God* (Hamden, Conn.: Archon Books, 1964), p. 7.
2. Daniel Day Williams, *The Spirit and Forms of Love* (New York: Harper and Row, 1968).